Pigskin DREAMS

THE PEOPLE, PLACES, AND EVENTS
THAT FORGED THE CHARACTER OF THE

NFL's Greatest Players

Dr. Stephen Below and Todd Kalis

Byrd and Bull Publishing
Clanton, Alabama
www.pigskindreams.com

Pigskin

DREAMS

ISBN: 978-0-615-31128-9 (paperback)
ISBN: 978-0-615-32758-7 (hardcover)
First Edition

Published by Byrd and Bull Publishing
507 2nd Avenue South, Clanton, AL 35045
1-866-596-9292

Please visit our web site at
www.pigskindreams.com.
Online ordering is available for all products.
For information, or bulk orders, contact info@pigskindreams.com
or call 1-866-596-9292.

Edited by Michael Garrett and Naomi Absher

Design and layout by Byrd and Bull Publishing
Cover design by Ginger Connell
Layout design by Amanda Parker

Printed in the United States of America
by Jostens Commercial Printing
State College, PA 16803 • 1-888-897-9693

Foreword

$\mathcal{O}$ ne of the core beliefs I have about winning is that a team wins with good people. If you have all the talent in the world on your team, and some of those players are lacking in the values you need to be successful, there's only so far a team can go. When it comes down to a critical moment in a game, if the character isn't there, you lose your edge. Talent takes you only so far, and when the going gets tough, it's the depth of character that provides that unique spark of excellence that is required to win. It's just as important as ability.

If you want to be successful, your team needs to consist of people with character who act according to the vision and values that are shared by the group. If you don't have that kind of environment, you're constantly distracted and drawn further away from your objective—further from the success you seek at any level. When you have core values and a common vision that guides the behavior of a group, then everyone in that group will begin to move in the same direction.

There is no easy walk to excellence. The best of the best know there is no such thing as a shortcut. All great results are built on the foundation of practice and preparation. The great athlete, student, parent, or business person might make what they do look easy, but they've invested so much energy and time in preparation it just appears that way. What they've actually done is *over learn* their particular skill to a level of excellence.

When you *over learn* a particular skill, you no longer have to think about performing that skill. Essentially, you're on autopilot. For example, a great running back has spent countless hours running drills, learning systems, and visualizing his anticipated performance. When he gets in a particular situation, the player is able to automatically adjust to changing circumstances—like a linebacker blitz—and react using the skills and abilities he's spent so much time developing. The better he's developed those skills, the better his outcome will be.

The same kind of thing happens in everyday life, too. The student who fastidiously applies him or herself to the subject at hand gains a greater understanding of the scholastic matter and creates an environment for higher understanding and opportunity. The parent who is steadfast in their constructive application of encouragement and correction sees the outcome of their efforts in the production of a well-adjusted, happy child that contributes to society. And the business-person who consistently applies and hones his or her business skills experiences greater success than those who do not take the time and effort to maximize those skills. *Over learning* creates an environment that allows a person to move to the next level, and it's a key ingredient to success in any endeavor.

The players included in *Pigskin Dreams* are perfect examples of people who understand the value of character. The character they possess is not just something they were born with or something that just magically appeared. Their character was developed from birth to where they are now—by the people, places, and events they encountered and by their estimation and reaction to those circumstances. All those influences can accurately be described as learning opportunities that illustrate the impact that teachers and coaches can have on the development of character. And when I use the terms teachers and coaches, I mean any person or circumstance that has the capacity to impart an influence on another person.

At just about any moment of time, what you say and what you do has the capacity to have a huge impact on people's lives. There's always an opportunity to participate in a "teaching moment" in someone's life. And it doesn't matter if you're a coach, parent, manager, or even a total stranger. At some level, we're all coaches—coaching players, coaching our kids, coaching employees, or advising friends. The dynamics and criteria are essentially the same.

Whether it's on the field of competition or in the kitchen of your own home, there's a coaching opportunity waiting to happen. The stories in *Pigskin Dreams* are wonderful illustrations of the impact good parenting and coaching can have on an individual. Behind every success story, whether it's success as a Hall of Fame football player, a student athlete, or an everyday guy with an attitude that he is going to do his job to the best of his abilities, there's always somebody in the background who had some positive influence on that person and helped them incorporate positive values into their lives.

As a football coach my objective was to win on game day—every game day. In order to have the opportunity to be in a position to win on game day required that the weeks and months before were filled with the proper preparation. With all the talent in the world, if our players didn't develop and use that talent in an optimal fashion on game day, our chances at success were greatly diminished. You've got to have a plan, you've got to execute your plan and you've got to do it with the right attitude, which is a by-product of the character values you've developed, if you want to be successful.

The players illustrated in *Pigskin Dreams* became the best of the best. In life, they exhibit the same winning characters that they brought on to the field. Their families, their acquaintances, their coaches, and their experiences combined to forge their character into winning individuals. There are numerous gems of wisdom in their stories that parents can take stock in to help them provide the leadership they need to help prepare their own kids for success in life, that kids can use to help them make successful choices, and that others can use to enrich their lives and the lives of others around them.

A dear old comedian, Red Skelton, perhaps described it best when he said, "If you have any talent, that's God's gift to you. If you use that talent, that's your gift to God." At any given moment, we all have the opportunity to decide whether we want to spend our time striving to be magnificent or just ordinary. And it doesn't matter if you're an athlete or not. Character provides the leverage necessary to move your life to higher potentials. The expectation of the leader—the parent, coach, or the manager—provides an important fulcrum to help others ascend to, and express their hidden potentials.

— *Coach Don Shula*

Contents

C o n t e n t s

Acknowledgments

Acknowledgments

$\mathcal{W}$e would like to thank the players for taking time out of their schedules to be interviewed for our book. True to form, when they understood our intention was to provide positive inputs for parents and kids, they took the time to share their stories and offer their insights to play a part in creating something constructive to help their fellow man. That's why they're winners.

Likewise, Coach Don Shula, who provided the foreword, Garth Brooks, Bob Costas, Roger Goodell, Art Rooney, and Bill Johnson, who provided jacket quotes, were gracious enough to contribute to our project. What you may not know about these men is that they all contribute their time and resources to other projects and programs to help other people. We are honored that they would participate and endorse our project.

Without the help of our attorney, Richard W. Rappaport, this project would likely have never materialized. We thank you for your guidance and advice. You pointed us in the right direction when we were spinning like a roulette wheel and kept pushing us forward.

To the many folks in the trenches who helped take an idea and turn it into reality, we want you to know how important you all were to the process. You all define the meaning of team. For the long hours of interview transcriptions, Kelli Smith was as good a partner as one could ever hope to associate with. The keen eyes and skills of our editors, Michael Garrett and Naomi Absher, brought more life to an already lively project.

Thanks to Gary Ernest for his exceptional skill in the electronic world. You are the bridge that crosses the river between the things we don't know that we don't know.

Ginger Connell and Amanda Parker deserve special thanks for their unwavering support and extraordinary skill that provided so much to this process. It's staggering to look back on all they have contributed and the level of talent that they provided. Among the many blessings we have in our lives, you are counted among them.

To all the folks who reviewed our work and offered constructive comments, we want you to know how important your input was.

To our friends, we cut our teeth together and learned about the world together. You inspired us, gave us direction, and stayed by our sides during the high and low tides of our lives. You made us better. We hope we've added something positive to your lives.

To our coaches who pushed us, expected more from us than we were aware we had to offer, and helped to teach us that accountability is like the boomerang of karma: if you throw it out into the universe, it comes back with commensurate force and intensity.

Thanks to Coach Gerald Johnson. A long forgotten, passing statement you made one day changed the course of a young man's life. Thanks for that. You made such a positive difference in the lives of so many kids.

To Coach Harold Pigusch, your sage advice provided me with the opportunity to explore my potential as a professional athlete. That day changed my life. Thank you for your unselfish guidance.

To J.L. Below, you were, and continue to be my hero. You set the bar high and that has always been my mark to aim for.

To Dottie Below, what a gift God gave us to share our lives with you. There were no better angels.

To Ron Kalis, your daily example provided the foundation of my character. I am what I am today due to the guidance you provided.

To Barb Kalis, the environment you created in our home gave me the strength to pursue my dreams, always.

To our kids, Casey, Josie, Buck, Talon, Kyle, Jennifer, and James, we hope the best of us provides a beacon for you to follow on your path. Your goals and aspirations are always one choice away. Your happiness is our greatest reward. Godspeed to all of you on your journey.

To Gina Below, you epitomize the cliché, "behind every successful man is a good woman." Without your love, support, and friendship, fewer things are possible and the world would not shine so bright.

To Kristen Kalis, you are the most giving person I have ever known. You are my best friend and your love gives me the power to be my best everyday.

Introduction

Introduction

*D*o we move through life, or does life move through us? How you answer that question determines what kind of life you live. For those who achieve success and happiness in life, the obvious answer is that life moves through them. They lasso their circumstance and consistently direct it toward a destination they envision, thereby creating a life in the image of their pursuits.

Conversely, many people simply move through life, spending the first half of their lives trying to learn how to live, and the last half of their lives learning how to die, often with little or no sense of accomplishment or purpose. Life happens to some, and some make life happen.

Pigskin Dreams: The People, Places, and Events that Forged the Character of the NFL's Greatest Players is a book about making life happen. It's a book full of stories that reveal the challenges, inspirations, lessons, and sacrifices that twenty-two Pro Football Hall of Fame players experienced on their road to greatness, on and off the field. It's a book full of "success gems" that every person who wants to be successful would benefit from exposure and incorporation into their own lives.

Pigskin Dreams is a collection of stories, based on personal interviews, about the early influences that helped to forge the character of these great players. And, while it is a book about football players, the messages they share with you go far beyond the gridiron. Their stories are about life and what it takes to achieve success in life.

Success qualities and patterns are portable. They tend to work in all the different areas of life that you pursue. While athletes might develop their skills and their character on the field, they take those qualities and apply them to other areas of their lives. What you become, what you are, is the constant shadow that follows you wherever you are. Character is your Siamese twin, bound forever to you, and destined to define you.

Character is a permanent fixture in your life, but it's also a ductile fixture, able to be shaped into new forms without being broken. Whether it's athletics, business, education, or relationships, your character transfers its value to all aspects of your life. We believe that the richer the character component is in your life, the richer your life will be.

Pigskin Dreams was born out of conversations between the authors about kids and how athletics has a definitive, positive impact on the development of character in them. Conversations ensued, time passed, and the idea to interview football greats, specific to our character theme, surfaced and became our plan, so we could share this information with parents, kids, coaches, fans, and others who would be interested in learning about some of the elements that made these players great.

Eight-year NFL veteran Todd Kalis conducted the interviews and brought an insider's look into the lives of these players. Having played in the NFL, Todd was part of a strong brotherhood and was graciously well received by all the interviewees. And when the players understood that our intention was to help promote values and character in our society, they were all the more willing to help us with this important project. It's simply another example of the contributions these great players lend and is one of many things they do to help improve the lot of their fellow man and woman.

Dr. Stephen Below edited the interviews, designed the format, and provided the commentaries and additional copy for the project. The entire project was a stellar example of what a team can accomplish when everyone contributes their particular area of expertise to the game.

The twenty-two players in *Pigskin Dreams* are wonderful examples of people who optimized their potential and achieved extraordinary success. Their stories provide a glimpse into their lives and reveal many of the circumstances and thought processes that helped them achieve the level of success they did. Their stories are not intended to be a comprehensive guide to becoming a professional football player, but for those who have such a goal, they will find valuable examples they can emulate to help them get closer to their goals. As is with anything, if you want to learn, learn from the best.

The stories are more accurately intended to provide examples of how a group of men came to be successful in their chosen profession, particularly relative to the influences they had as children and young adults. The basic criteria for success in life remain essentially the same, regardless of the endeavor you undertake. Their challenges, intentions, commitment, sacrifice, failures, and victories combine to define their journeys and destinies, to provide you with an inside look at what success looks like and what it takes to achieve success.

For parents, *Pigskin Dreams* is a book that we hope will provide insights to help and encourage them to stress the importance of good character in their children—through their attention, advice, and example. Share this book with your kids. Read them the stories and talk about the circumstances that each player faced, how many overcame great challenges, and how all became what they are, ultimately, through the efforts they expended. Talk to your kids about right choices, hard work, and reward, and help them understand that great things require great effort, and that accomplishment of great things produces the greatest happiness and fulfillment. You're the coach, and practice happens every day, rain or shine. The better you prepare your team members, the better their lives will be.

For young men and women who will read this book, we hope they find many examples of success that will resonate with them. For the younger folks who have a desire to achieve great things in their lives, our greatest reward would be in having the opportunity to play a small part in achieving your dreams and aspirations. Now is the time for you to be laying the foundation for your success and developing the character required to attain success and happiness in your life. You're truly the masters of your destinies, and your ships will sail to where you steer them. Chart your course, choose wisely, act accordingly, and life holds rewards beyond your wildest expectations. If you can dream it and believe it, you can do it.

For coaches, there are a vast array of observations, examples, attitudes, and outcomes in this book that they can draw from to help them be even more effective, not only as a coach, but as a difference-maker in the lives of their players and students. At the end of the day, we suspect that you take as much, or more, satisfaction from the positive impact you have on a kid as you do in assisting a gifted player to get a college scholarship. Your greatest gifts are those lessons you pass on to the kids who cross your path, because those are the things of value and character that kids will take with them as they go into the world to make their marks and offer their contributions.

For fans, these stories will provide an even deeper sense of attachment to the game and the players that they love. What were some of the critical events and influences that helped these players become the best of the best? You'll find some of the answers in their stories and capture a newfound appreciation for the commitment it required for these players to achieve the status that they did.

There are two main messages about success that lurk within the lines of this book. One is external, the other internal. The external component is illustrated through the environment these players grew up in. Their parents, neighbors, coaches, teachers, and others played critical roles in helping the players develop the winning characters that they did. These people created an environment for these players that laid a firm foundation for their character, from which they built their stellar careers. Without all those wonderful, solid influences, history may have taken a much different route for many of these players.

The internal component is the element of choice. Throughout the book, choice becomes a critical factor in the progression of the players' careers and lives. While the culmination of their careers may best be illustrated through their induction into the Pro Football Hall of Fame, the events that led to that were the choices these players made long ago. With their strong foundations, the players were better equipped to make the right choices that paved the road to their success.

There are two other things we hope you, the reader, will absorb from this book. First, is the realization that you have the ability to make a tremendous difference in other peoples' lives. Maybe it's a child, a friend, or a total stranger, but never discount the impact you can have on another's life through what you say, think, or do. You never know how far-reaching a helpful gesture or bit of advice might be. You may just provide the instruction or example to lay the foundation for the next football star, president, doctor, or outstanding parent. You just have to remember that you can make a difference.

The other thing would refer to your own character. We never reach the pinnacle of perfect character. It's something we constantly have to practice and keep in our mind as our intended way to live our lives. In fact, from its Greek origin, character means to mark or engrave upon. There are so many things in our lives, good and bad, that have left their marks on us. Our estimations of those things create our character, and it's never too late to begin a new direction in life, if you're willing to consistently incorporate additional positive elements into your life. Character is simply the mark you've embraced and given your attention to. If you're not satisfied with your current situation, add some new "marks" to serve as the channel for life to move through you, in its highest expression, commensurate with the intentions and actions that you provide to create your destiny.

Thank you for allowing us the opportunity to share our work with you. We hope you find as much value and fun in reading it as we did in compiling it.

For the best in all of us,
Dr. Steve and Todd

Chapter 1

BOBBY BELL

*"If you want to be respected by others, the great thing
is to respect yourself. Only by that, only by self-respect,
will you compel others to respect you."*
— ***Fyodor Dostoevsky***

Robert "Bobby" Bell, Jr. was born on June 17, 1940, in Shelby,
North Carolina. Bobby Bell excelled at several sports at
Cleveland High School in Shelby. He started his high school
career as a freshman halfback on a six-man team. In his junior year
the school switched to an eleven-man team, and Bell quickly became
an all-state quarterback.

Bell was so outstanding at quarterback that the coach at North Carolina University, Jack Tatum, wanted no part of Bell as an opponent.
Coach Tatum knew that Notre Dame and Michigan State were both
interested in recruiting Bell, and those schools were on North Carolina's schedule, so Tatum contacted Denver Crawford, a coach at the
University of Minnesota, and told him about the rare talents of Bell.
Because Cleveland High School could not afford to film their games,
Bell became the first scholarship player to be accepted sight unseen
at Minnesota in 1959.

As a freshman at Minnesota, Bell was the first-string quarterback,
but a shortage of quality tackles prompted Minnesota Coach Murray
Warmath to shift Bell to tackle early in his sophomore season.

Coach Warmath told Bell that he was going to be an All-American
tackle in the next year or two, which Bell didn't believe. Bobby didn't
even know how to get in a lineman's stance, but he did end up as an

All-American tackle his junior and senior years, and in 1962 won the Outland Trophy as the nation's top lineman.

Bell was drafted by the Kansas City Chiefs in 1963 and started his professional career as a defensive end. By Bobby's third season with the Chiefs, Bell made the permanent move to linebacker, where he developed into super-stardom, winning either All-AFC or All-AFL designations during the next eight seasons. During that period, Bell starred on two AFL championship teams, played in Super Bowls I and IV, and was named to the last six AFL All-Star games and the first three AFC-NFC Pro Bowl contests. In 1969, he was selected to the all-time AFL team.

At 6'4" and 228 pounds, Bell was built like an inverted pyramid, with massive shoulders and a 32-inch waist. He consistently ran the 40-yard dash in 4.5 seconds, and Coach Hank Stram of Kansas City commented, "You hear a lot about all-around football players, but you don't really see many. There isn't a job Bell couldn't do and do well. He could play all twenty-two positions on the field and play them well. Attitude-wise, Bobby was a rookie all the years he played for us. I think if you had a team full of Bobby Bells, you'd want to coach forever, and you'd win forever."

Bell was inducted into the Kansas City Hall of Fame in 1980 and the Professional Football Hall of Fame in 1983. His number (78) was retired by the Kansas City Chiefs. He was ranked number 66 on *The Sporting News'* list of the 100 Greatest Football Players in 1999.

66 **I** was born in North Carolina, and I've got one older brother and one older sister. I'm the baby, and my mom always called me the baby.

"I grew up in the South—the cotton gin, cotton milling part of the South where they turned cotton into yarn and yarn into cloth. My dad worked for the Double Mill Textile Mill, and my mother worked at home washing clothes, cleaning the house, and taking care of us kids.

"Most of the people that worked at the mills lived around the mills. It was like a suburb of the company. Some of the mills had their own schools, their own stores, and their own churches, and they would build homes around the mills for the workers.

"My dad worked for the mills since he was about fifteen or sixteen years old, and my family still owns the old house by the mill my dad worked at.

"The house burned down once when I was about six years old. I almost burned down with it! My mother was out hanging up clothes to dry, and I was inside taking a nap. We had a wood-burning stove in the house. Somehow it started the house on fire.

"So, the house is burning—with me in it—and people are saying, *Where are the kids?* And my mother is screaming, *Where's my baby? Where's my baby?* Somebody said, *He's in the house!* So, the house is almost completely in flames and my mother is hollering, and the people there are holding her and not letting her go in the house. Finally, they let her loose when she told them she was okay. As soon as they let her go, she broke for the front door.

"She couldn't see anything because of all the smoke in the house. I remember her grabbing me by the leg and pulling me out of the house, and I guess when she pulled me off the bed I woke up when my head hit the floor, and I started crying as she was dragging me out of the house. The only things that were saved were the clothes on the clothesline outside, a radio somebody reached into the window and got, and me!

"The people my dad worked for came through for us after our loss. They rebuilt the house for free. And other neighbors and friends gave us clothes and pulled together as a kind of family. That helped us bounce back.

"Growing up, I had some good, sound foundations that my parents imparted to us kids. We went to church every week. We had chores to do, we earned all the money that we had to spend, and our dad made sure that we paid for whatever we got.

"We didn't really have all the sports and stuff that kids have today when I was growing up. Back in my day, what we had was a guy named Flip Wilson. That was really his name.

"Flip Wilson had a dream of starting a boys club for the black kids. When I was a kid, black kids went to black schools and white kids went to white schools. I had friends who were white, but everything was separate. We had separate parks, separate sections where you could sit in a theater, separate places to do most things. So, Flip came up with the idea of a boys club.

"Flip went out and raised some money and started the Shelby Sports Club. He found a bus and painted the name of the club on the side. He would pick up all the kids, and we would play basketball and baseball. We all went out and begged for donations, and people would donate uniforms and other equipment. Parents chipped in and had rallies and things like that.

"So, that's how we started it off and where I began my athletic experience. And, I learned something very fundamental back then. I learned that there's only one way of doing things—the right way.

"All the parents were involved in the boys club, and they were all on the same wavelength about how kids should act. If anybody got out of line, Flip, or one of the other parents, had the authority to punish them. If you were bad enough, one of the other parents would give you a whipping. That made all of us kids walk a straighter line.

"If any parents in the neighborhood saw you acting up, they would come up and say, *Hey, you know your mom won't let you do that, straighten up!* That's just the way everybody felt around here. If you were too bad out of line, Flip would call your parents and tell them that you were out of the club until you did certain things to rectify the situation.

"I didn't get too many whippings when I was young. But I remember one time at elementary school when the principal came up to me and said that I was doing something I wasn't supposed to be doing. He said he was going to give me some swats, and I was asking him why he did that. I was arguing with him and told him I was going to go home and tell my dad.

"Later, I told my dad he wasn't going to believe this, but the principal spanked me because he thought I was playing with a girl's hair. My dad didn't even say one word. He went into the other room, then came back—with his belt. He whipped me again.

"I asked my dad why I was getting another whipping. He told me that the principal must not have done a good enough job the first time. That's the kind of upbringing I got, and I got the point.

"If I acted up, it was on me—so don't expect any sympathy if you come home complaining about getting yourself in trouble. The parents, teachers, and neighbors all had that kind of relationship in my community. Our community was close and tight. Everybody looked out for everybody else.

"I grew up in a pretty competitive environment. My brother played sports also, and we were in competition with each other all of the time. But all of the kids in the neighborhood were competitive. Everybody gave 120 percent because they wanted to be a standout player, too.

"We played six-man football in high school. I was the quarterback, and my brother was an end. They called us the Bell brothers. As the quarterback, I just naturally wanted to throw the ball to my brother as often as I could.

"My brother was a rough and tough kind of guy. He believed he could do anything in the world. No one could out jump him and nobody could out run him. He was good enough to have played college and professional football. He could have done it all.

"Growing up, our neighborhood was like a suburb of the mill. It was its own little community. I learned how to play with the white kids in the community, but by the time I was twelve or thirteen I realized a little more about the racial side of things.

"We would go to town, and it really didn't bother us, but we had to go to separate bathrooms and drink out of the water fountain for the blacks. And there were certain restaurants you couldn't eat in. When I went to college in Minnesota, it was an entirely different environment there.

"I guess I was about twelve when I first started playing any kind of organized sport. That was with the boys club that Flip Wilson started, and we played football, baseball and basketball.

"Flip would have been the person who had the most influence on me to play sports. He wanted to get all the young kids involved in sports. He would haul us all over the place and get us involved in the fundamentals of the sports.

"Flip never played sports himself, but he had knowledge of sports. He organized, disciplined, and taught us about the fundamentals. He had a vision.

"My mom didn't really know that much about sports. She was kind of preoccupied with taking care of us kids and the house. But my dad was a big fan. My dad was a big believer that if you worked hard, you could achieve anything you wanted to.

"I used to go with my dad to help him take care of the yards at the country club. I got to know some of the white kids who lived there. A lot of them went to private schools, and I got to look at one of their yearbooks one time.

"I was pretty impressed by the school they were attending and re-member telling my dad that I'd do anything to be able to go to a big school like the one in the yearbook. He told me that if I worked hard, that it was possible. He didn't have too many words to say, but when he spoke, it really stuck with me.

"My dad always looked at me as a baseball player. I was really better at baseball than at football. When I was a junior in high school, I had a chance to go play with the Chicago White Sox in their farm league. They had come down to watch us play, and they wanted to sign me.

"The guy from the White Sox came and talked to my dad and told him that he thought I could be one of the greatest baseball players ever, and that the Sox would like to sign me. My dad told him it was up to me.

"When the guy from Chicago left, my dad said that all I ever talked about was going to school. My dad never even finished elementary school, and he told me that if I signed, I would never finish school. He said you could never go back and get that opportunity.

"I told him that I could sign, make some money, and come back later and finish school. He told me that he didn't think I'd ever do that. He thought that if I went out and started making money, I'd never go back to school. That was good, common sense advice.

"So, I decided to stay in high school. I had people telling me I was pretty good, and I thought I could get a scholarship to help pay for a college education. I ended up getting a football scholarship at the University of Minnesota.

"The University of Minnesota called our high school to get some films of me to look at. But our high school was so poor it didn't have any film equipment, so I ended up at another high school running some speed tests and doing some workouts. The workout went well, and Minnesota sent me a plane ticket to come visit the school and ultimately offered me their last scholarship.

"So, my dream was coming true. I was going to get to go to a big school like I had always wanted to. There were more students at the University of Minnesota than there were people in the county I lived in North Carolina. I remember calling my dad and telling him this is where I want to go, even though it was a long way from home. My dad always told me if I worked hard, I could accomplish my goals. He was right!

"At the time, Minnesota had the best college baseball team in the country, and I was excited about the possibility of playing football and baseball. I asked the football coach if I could play baseball and football, and he told me I could. But I never did get to play baseball there. Every year the coach would tell me, *Maybe next year*. I did get to play basketball at Minnesota, though. I was the first black kid to ever play basketball there.

"There were a lot of people back in my hometown who tried to encourage me to stay closer to home and not go all the way to Minnesota because it was so far away. I remember a teacher and assistant coach I had, Coach Henry, would always take time with me and talk to me. He encouraged me to go to Minnesota and told me I was strong enough to do it and had the willpower to do it. He told me that it would be hard, but that nothing worthwhile was easy, and he really believed in me and let me know that I could do it.

"When I first started playing football, a lot of people said I was too small. When I was younger, I was always the small guy, the runt. Coach Henry always encouraged me, even in elementary school. He always encouraged me and told me I could play, that I could do it, and not to worry about what everybody else was saying. Even when so many people were telling me I shouldn't go to Minnesota, Coach Henry was telling me I should because I had the biggest dreams, the greatest willpower, desire, and pride of anybody he'd ever known.

"Coach Henry, and my head coach, Coach Winston, helped instill in me the desire to win. I remember Coach Henry saying, *Bobby, anytime you walk off the field, look in the mirror and ask yourself if you gave 110 percent today. If you can't say yes, you've shorted yourself today.* Coach Winston would say, *When you walk off that field and your opponent doesn't say that Bobby Bell was the toughest opponent he's played against today, you haven't done your job.* That stuck with me through high school, college, and the pros. When I put my uniform on, even if I was a little banged up, I was there to give it everything I had—every ounce. You were going to know I was there. My team could count on me.

"I think that attitude, the attitude of giving your best effort, is a reflection of my background. My parents and the people I was surrounded by cared about me as a person. And I had a desire to do things right. I didn't want to do something wrong because it would let so many people down—my parents, my coaches, my friends, and my community. I had pride in myself, and I wanted other people to have pride in me, too.

"That desire I had, and all the good influences, had a lot to do with the kind of character I had. There were guys who were better athletes than I was, but they would just give up at some point. If they got knocked down a time or two, it's like some of them just folded up. Not me. To me it was a dog fight all day long, and if you knocked me down a few times, I was going to get back up every time. I was going to give you all I had.

"All those traits came from my mom and dad. They never quit, and they didn't sell themselves short. And others had an influence on that, too, like Flip Wilson and The Shelby Sports Club. He would tell us if we couldn't give it our all, don't even show up, don't even put on the uniform, and don't even bother coming through the door. And my high school coach would tell us if we didn't want to play, don't even bother showing up and wasting his time. We lived with a level of expectation around us that if we were going to show up, we better show up with our best effort.

"In high school we only had seven total players on our basketball team. We won the state championship. We showed up to play, and we were in better shape than any other team. We ran and ran and never stopped running. That was back in the fifties, and it wasn't unusual for us to score 100 points or more in a game. I remember our high school team used to have practice games with a local junior college. We would wear them out.

"That's the way it was for us. We came to play. That was just our *normal*. We had people coming from all over the state to watch us play basketball and football—whites and blacks. We were very disciplined and respectful kids—respectful of our parents, our coaches, and the people around us. And there were people in the community keeping an eye on us all the time. If you got in trouble, you knew it wouldn't be long till somebody told your mom or your dad what you did. People don't do that anymore.

"A few years ago Darrell Porter, the great Kansas City Royals catcher, and I went to a high school to talk to the kids there. Darrell got up to speak first, and it was sad to see how disrespectful those kids were. They were playing cards, talking, cutting up, and just generally being disrespectful. When I got up to speak, I apologized to Darrell for the disrespect these kids were showing. And it was like the kids didn't really even care, because they knew if they got disciplined by the teachers that all they had to do was complain to the right person and the teacher would be the one who's in trouble. Kids today just don't seem to have the kind of values we were brought up with.

"I think by the time I was about twelve years old I had my values in place. From there, I think you just continue to develop and incorporate those values into your life. My parents were the primary influences on me, but it didn't stop there. Every time you walked out of the house in my neighborhood, there were all the other parents out there keeping an eye on you and disciplining you, too. There was a feeling of accountability in that neighborhood. I was accountable for my actions, and I understood that doing the wrong stuff carried a penalty. But even more than that, I felt accountable to everybody around there. I wanted them to be proud of me, and I wanted to earn their respect.

"As far as any advice I have for parents today, I'd say the most important thing is just to love your kids. Tell them you love them every day. Show them respect, and show them how to respect you, too. There are so many kids today who disrespect their parents. Respect is just such an important thing.

"I remember, when I was about seventeen, I was a pretty strong kid, and I was pretty quick. You know, at seventeen I thought I was pretty tough and that I could whip anybody in town. I was fooling around with my dad one day out in the yard, kind of grabbing at him and telling him that I could wear him out.

"That's when he grabbed me and put me to the ground and got real close to me and said, *Don't you ever mess with me like that, you hear?* It didn't take me too long to say, Yes Sir! My dad was like cement block. He was strong, and there I was on the ground thinking that he was going to kill me! If I had briefly forgotten a little about respect, it only took me a second or two to get reacquainted with it that day.

"Parents have to love their kids, give them the right foundation, and instill the proper morals. You have to do that every day, and when there's a problem, you have to correct it. And don't wait three or four days to correct the problem, because then the parent gets in the bad habit of letting things go that should be dealt with at the present time. As long as your kids are in your house, the parents have to take a hands-on approach to raising those kids. You have to be consistent, and you have to deal with issues when they arise, because you might not get the chance again."

* * *

I n the 1976 film, *The Shootist,* John Wayne utters one of his most famous lines, "I won't be wronged, I won't be insulted, and I won't be laid a hand upon. I don't do these things to other people and I expect the same from them."

Respect, the esteem or worth you feel for another person (or yourself), is one of the critical cornerstones of character. One of the unique things about respect is that the more of it you give, the more of it you receive.

Respect is like the fuel that powers your car—keep the tank full and your journey opens up to many more potential opportunities. Conversely, if you don't keep a fresh supply of fuel in your respect tank, you tend to get hung up in the traffic of life and don't make much progress.

Respecting yourself is prerequisite to showing respect to others. There's a certain amount of dignity and self-value that you must possess about yourself, and that self-image begins forming at birth, through your particular environment and the influences your environment provides. Living honorably and authentically sustains and increases your levels of self-respect and provides you with a source of inner strength and autonomy.

The dictionary describes respect as a noun. But respect is really more like a verb, because respect requires action. One must actively engage in respecting fellow human beings through the positive attentions and actions that are given to others. Respect is the first step you take and provides the momentum you maintain on the road to your destiny.

As a practical, hypothetical example, imagine a young high school football coach in his first head coaching position. The coach has worked hard and wants to succeed at his new position. But this coach forgot a little about respect and started berating and humiliating his players because they weren't winning ball games. One night he even made them run sprints after a losing game, in front of all the fans in attendance.

The coach crossed a line that night and mistook humiliating his players for positive correction. That night the coach disrespected his team and lost the respect of his team and the fans. He replaced his self-respect with contempt, born from his inability to produce the results he desired.

Respect breeds respect. It nourishes itself from its own processes and dynamics. Bobby Bell understood that and applied it to his professional and personal life. He gave respect to others, and he got respect back, and perhaps one of the greatest compliments he ever got was from his coach, Hank Stram, when he said, "I think if you had a team full of Bobby Bells, you'd want to coach forever, and you'd win forever." You don't get those kinds of accolades without respect.

Chapter 2

MEL   BLOUNT

*A person will worship something, have no doubt about
that. That which dominates our imaginations and our
thoughts will determine our lives, and our character.
Therefore, it behooves us to be careful what we worship,
for what we are worshiping we are becoming.*
— Ralph Waldo Emerson

Melvin Cornell Blount was born April 10, 1948, in Vidalia,
Georgia. He was the youngest of eleven children and grew
up in poverty in a home without plumbing or electricity.
Blount excelled in football, basketball, baseball, and track at Lyons
High School. He received a football scholarship to Southern University in Baton Rouge, Louisiana, and was selected all-conference SWAC
team twice and was the SWAC Most Valuable Player in his junior
year. In the spring of 1970, the Pittsburgh Steelers selected him in the
third round of the NFL draft as the fifty-third overall pick.

Blount played for fourteen years in Pittsburgh (1970-1983) and
helped the Steelers achieve four Super Bowl victories. Blount made
the Pro Bowl five times and was the Pro Bowl MVP in 1977. He won
the NFL Defensive Player of the Year Award in 1975 and was a four-
time All-Pro selection. As a defensive back, Blount finished his career
with fifty-seven interceptions, thirteen fumble recoveries, and two
touchdowns. He also returned thirty-six kickoffs for 911 yards. He
played in 200 games and missed only one game over the course of his
fourteen seasons in the NFL.

During his last season with the Steelers, he and his brother opened the Mel Blount Youth Home in Vidalia, Georgia, to assist boys who are victims of abuse or neglect. He also opened a second boys' home in 1989 at his home in Claysville, Pennsylvania, and continues as an advocate for troubled boys.

Mel Blount is an accomplished horseman and won the open division of the 1990 cutting horse championship at the Florida Cutting Horse Association Show. He was inducted into the World Sports Humanitarian Hall of Fame in 1997. In 1990, he was inducted into the Georgia Sports Hall of Fame. In 1989, he was inducted into the Pro Football Hall of Fame and the Louisiana Sports Hall of Fame. In 1994, he was named to the NFL's 75th anniversary All-Time Team and was ranked number 36 on *The Sporting News'* list of the 100 Greatest Football Players.

66 **I** was born in Vidalia, Georgia, on a farm about eight miles outside of town. It was definitely country, and we lived out in the woods. I was the youngest of eleven kids. There were four girls and seven boys. We were country when country wasn't cool. Our closest neighbor was a little over a mile away. My folks were basically dirt farmers. Sharecropping was a common way of life in the South at that time. But a significant part of my story is that my parents owned their own land. That wasn't something you commonly saw, black and poor people owning their land.

"We [the kids] were the work force for the farm. We were the ones helping to grow and harvest the crops. We did a lot of that. Everybody in the family was involved with the farm work—my dad, my mom, and all the kids. If you lived out in the country in those days, you basically lived off the land.

"We had a very stable family with two great parents. The atmosphere was secure and very conducive to raising a family. There were no distractions like seeing other people on drugs or alcohol, because back in those days we didn't know anything like that existed. It was a nice upbringing and a critical component of who I am.

"We were very sheltered, my brothers, sisters, and I. We grew up in the segregated South, and our parents sheltered us from that. They protected us, and we drew strength from our parents. They were good, strong role models for us—good Christian people, and to tell you the truth, a lot of who I am today is a result of my parents teaching us to respect and love other people.

"When people would get sick, I can remember my parents visiting them at their homes and staying up with them until late at night. Then my folks would get home late, go to bed, get up early and work all day. And they would do this until the sick person either got well or passed away. So, a lot about who I am and what I'm doing today is a result of how I saw my family really reach out to people in the community to help nurture and care for other people. We were very grounded because we had family, church, community, and a strong work ethic. We had some basic fundamental principles that shaped our lives.

"I remember how my parents would always tell us to treat people the way we wanted to be treated. That saying really stuck with me. And, as far as our work ethic was concerned, my dad would always say, *Early to bed, early to rise makes a man healthy, wealthy, and wise.* If you go to bed early and get up early, while everybody else is asleep, you're out there working and getting ahead. Things like that and things like *Wise men are men who put God first* are a few of the basic principles that were instilled into us as kids.

"My parents didn't really play much of a role in my athletic career. My dad always wanted us to come home after school to work, instead of staying at school and practicing football. In fact, sometimes my dad would tell us that we couldn't stay for practice because he needed us to come home. But by the time I was a senior in high school, my dad was a little more lenient about sports. He didn't ever dream that his son would have a future in football, but when I came home from college for Christmas my freshman year, I think he finally realized that sports were giving me a tremendous opportunity—at least for an education. I'm glad he lived long enough to see that.

"My siblings were involved in high school sports, too. Sometimes it was a competitive atmosphere around our house, but it was also a nurturing atmosphere. The older kids really nurtured the younger ones and took care of them—loved them, disciplined them, and just made sure we stayed in line with what the program or system was within the family.

"I didn't really participate in any organized sport until the beginning of my sophomore year in high school. One of the biggest influences I had to play sports happened one day when I went to a neighbor's house. We didn't have a television at my house, but that particular day I saw the Baltimore Colts on the TV at my friend's house. That really got my interest, and that's when I went out for football in high school. My older brothers were really influential in my deciding to go into sports, too. They were very good athletes and good role models for me. My older brothers are probably the ones who got me paying attention to sports. I really enjoyed watching them play sports.

"I remember when Gale Sayers was setting records in Chicago when I was a sophomore in college. There was a bright kid in college with me named Adolpheus Denard. He always brought the newspaper in with him, and he would read about Gale Sayers and talk about how many touchdowns he made. That started getting my interest.

"In high school I had a coach named Jimmy Thacker who would bring in articles about a player he had coached who went on to play college football. Just about every Monday the coach would read about that player and what this kid had done in a game. I was just a kid from the country, but I remember thinking that one day the coach was going to be reading about Mel Blount scoring a touchdown or winning. Those kinds of stories really motivated and influenced me, and that's what it's all about—dreams and visualization—just putting yourself at that moment.

"As I look back at my career, I'd say that the moment I realized that sports could be a more serious opportunity occurred during my senior year in high school in a game against Meadow, Georgia. I ended up scoring five touchdowns in that game. Then, all of a sudden, colleges started contacting our principal and coaches wanting to find out more about me. So, I ended up with several college scholarship offers. That's when I started to realize that there were people out there who saw value in me, where I could help or contribute to their athletic program.

"But even with all the attention I was getting at the high school and college level, I didn't really take football too seriously. It was about my third or fourth year in the NFL when I really started taking football seriously. I saw college football more as an opportunity to get an education. Really, I was just young and immature. I was still adjusting as a person, because my entire background had been just dealing with black people. I didn't have the exposure to learn how to socially fit in or develop my communication skills. I was always a guy who was friendly and loved people, but I was also learning how to make some serious adjustments in my life, too. I was only twenty-one when I went into the NFL—a young and immature kid with some talent. Thank God Coach Knoll was patient enough to wait for me to develop.

"Looking back on my years at Pittsburgh, I can't really say there were any specific things that someone said or did that finally flipped a switch to help me grow as a player and an individual. It was really more about how the coaches were patient with me and how they worked with me day in and day out. It was like one day it just hit me, and the light came on. I understood that this was a profession and in order to succeed, you're going to have to be as competitive as you can be. You're going to have to show that you're of value to the organization, because if you don't, you won't be around for long. By that point, I think I had matured a good deal, and that's when I started taking the game more seriously.

"I think there are a lot of reasons why one person will succeed at what they do and another, with equal skills, may not. First of all, I think a person has to be grounded. I think my upbringing had a lot to do with me being able to survive the temptations of pro sports—the freedoms, the money, the fame, and celebrity that people place upon you. Just being grounded and having had a good upbringing was a critically important thing as far as my success as a player and an individual.

"I've seen a lot of guys who came into training camp who had as much, if not more, skill than I did. But it's a funny thing. It's a very small thread that separates those who make it and those who don't. And I think those who do make it are people who genuinely want something more out of life and are willing to work and sacrifice for it. I think those people who don't get what they want are either people who don't know how to pay the price to get it, or they're not willing to pay the price.

"It's different levels of satisfaction and commitment. All some guys may want to do is say they made the team. In their minds they've succeeded. Other guys take the attitude that they want to be the best player on the team, and that's a big difference. One has to know what kind of outcome they want to achieve, and they have to understand the levels of commitment and sacrifice that go along with achieving their goals. You can't just say you want to do something and expect it to happen. You have to put in the extra effort and commitment to accomplish extraordinary things.

"Of course, that doesn't always mean that you'll be completely satisfied with your performance. I can remember looking back at game films and thinking about how I could have done this or that better. Maybe I had two or three interceptions in a game and I'd say, Man, if I'd only caught that ball I could have had four! Or there may have been some critical blocks or tackles and you're thinking, Oh man, I should have done this or done that! I think that just about anybody who participates in higher levels of organized sports, or business for that matter, has this kind of attitude. You know, you always see where you could have made improvement and done just a little better. Nobody is really harder on yourself than yourself when it comes to critiquing your performance.

"I think a huge part of what we accomplish as adults starts early on with the value systems that we develop as kids. I think these value systems start pretty early on in life. I don't know exactly what age that might be, but I think what happens is that from these core values, one begins to critique their value systems and begins to realize where it is they want to go in life and what direction they're going to choose. I see that kind of thing with the kids I've been working with for so many years. You just can't wait until you're fourteen or fifteen years old to start developing some value systems and morals. It has to start from the day you're born. It's based on their upbringing and their nurturing and the tutoring they get from their parents that really shapes and molds them to be who they're ultimately going to be, or not be.

"One of the key things we do at the Mel Blount Youth Home is just to sit and listen to the kids. We listen to them, then we talk about what we heard them say. We try to help them work through the maze of whatever it is they're struggling with. See, that's critical with anyone, even as an adult. When you're going through things and you can go to somebody and you know they're listening to you and concerned about you, it releases the assurance that you've been able to share what you're going through with somebody. When you know some-body has heard you, it's like something that releases pressure off of you. Even though they might not be able to help you solve your prob-lem, at least you've had somebody to talk to. I think that's critical with kids, because most times as adults we're talking to kids instead of listening to them.

"As far as any advice I might give parents, I would say first to just let your kids know that you support them. Give them the tools to start making good, sound decisions, and leave the door open for them to start doing that, without the parent having to make the decision for them. As far as participation in sports, I'm not going to make my kids play anything they don't want to participate in. Sure, I'll tell them the pros and cons of playing a sport, but I'm not going to push them to participate if they don't want to.

"I want to give my kids the best information I can so they can start making their own decisions when the time is right. For example, if my kids were fortunate enough to get a scholarship, I wouldn't try to tell them what school to go to. They have to be the one to excel and succeed when they get there, not me. Plus, I wouldn't want them saying that they only made this choice because their daddy wanted them to go here or do that. Your kids have to be accountable for their choices at some point. That's the whole point of raising them, isn't it? To give them the best information and be the best example you can so they'll have the tools to make the right choices. And if you listen to them, you'll know if you've been doing a good job."

* * *

There is an ancient Greek myth about a shepherd recounted by Plato in his best-known work *The Republic*. During a severe thunderstorm a violent earthquake ripped open the earth and created a huge chasm where the shepherd was tending his sheep. With awe and curiosity, the shepherd climbed down into the chasm and, among the many marvelous objects he saw, was a hollow bronze horse. Beyond that, the shepherd could see a giant-sized corpse with nothing but a gold ring on one of its fingers. The shepherd pulled the ring off of the corpse, put it on his own finger, and climbed out of the chasm.

At a regular monthly meeting with other shepherds and the king, the shepherd turned the ring upside-down on his finger and, upon doing so, immediately became invisible.

After testing the ring several times, the shepherd came to realize the ring's power, and he proceeded to take full advantage of that power. The shepherd schemed to become one of the king's personal liaisons. He committed adultery with the king's wife, and subsequently, with the help of the king's wife, murdered the king and took over the kingdom of Lydia.

In *The Republic*, Glaucon, Socrates' brother, raised the question, if human beings could do whatever they wanted, without any consequence of being seen by others, what would human beings be like and what would they do?

It has been said that character is what you are in the dark, when no one else is around to see what you do. So, what ultimately makes you what you are? Aristotle says, "We are what we repeatedly do," and by no small measure, those things that we repeatedly do are based on the exposures and influences we've had in our lives.

While Mel Blount certainly didn't have the riches, comforts, and advantages that many people have growing up, he did repeatedly receive some basic and fundamental principles in a nurturing environment. These principles had a lot to do with his success as a professional football player, and they had everything to do with his success as a human being. In the dark, Mel Blount's character continues to shine. In fact, his character illuminates the lives of many others as he continues to do the things he has repeatedly done.

Chapter 3

DICK BUTKUS

The thing always happens that you really believe in;
and the belief in a thing makes it happen.
— Frank Lloyd Wright

Richard Marvin "Dick" Butkus was born on December 9, 1942, to Lithuanian immigrant parents in Chicago, Illinois. He was the youngest of nine children. The family lived in the Roseland section of Chicago's South Side.

Butkus attended high school at Chicago Vocational School, where he was a star football player. Along with his three teammates and life-long friends, dubbed the *Ferocious Quartet,* he was already developing a reputation as a hard-hitting, aggressive football player.

Dick Butkus played college football at the University of Illinois from 1962 through 1964 at the center and linebacker positions. In 1963 and 1964 he was unanimously named an All-American. He won the Chicago Tribune Silver Football in 1963 as the Big Ten Most Valuable Player and was named the American Football Coaches Association Player of the Year in 1964. He finished sixth in Heisman Trophy balloting in 1963 and third in 1964, a remarkable achievement given his defensive position as linebacker.

Butkus was inducted into the College Football Hall of Fame in 1983 and is only one of two players in the history of the University of Illinois to have his number (50) retired. The other player was Harold "Red" Grange. Butkus was also named to the Walter Camp All-Century Team in 1990 and was named as the sixth best college football player ever by *College Football News* in 2000. Perhaps the ultimate tribute was in

1985 when the Downtown Athletic Club of Orlando, Florida, created an award in his name, The Dick Butkus Award, which is given annually to the most outstanding linebacker in college football.

Dick Butkus was drafted in the first round of the NFL Draft by the Denver Broncos and the Chicago Bears. He played for the Bears from 1965 to 1973, when he was forced to retire due to multiple knee injuries. While playing middle linebacker for the Bears, he was selected to the Pro Bowl for eight seasons and was All-Pro six times.

As a rookie with the Bears, he led the team in tackles, interceptions, forced fumbles, and fumble recoveries, and regularly led the team throughout his career in these categories. In 1967, team statistics report that the one-man wrecking crew was involved in 867 of 880 defensive plays, leading the team with 111 solo tackles, thirty-five assists, and eighteen quarterback sacks. During his career, Butkus intercepted twenty-two passes and recovered twenty-five opponents' fumbles, an NFL record at the time of his retirement in 1973. During his professional career, he amassed 1,020 solo tackles and 489 assists.

Butkus was fierce on the football field. His opponents feared him, and his teammates respected him. Green Bay Packers running back MacArthur Lane said, "If I had a choice, I'd sooner go one-on-one with a grizzly bear. I prayed that I could get up every time Butkus hit me." Dick's teammate Doug Buffone observed, "I always say to play professional football, you have to have a Neanderthal gene. Dick had two." Baltimore trainer, Ernie Accorsi, remembers walking into a training room littered with injured players after one Bears-Colts game. He shrugged and offered a one-word explanation, "Butkus."

The Butkus legacy includes being selected as the 70th greatest athlete of the twentieth century by ESPN, the ninth best player in league history by *The Sporting News*, and the fifth best player of all time by the Associated Press. The NFL named him to their All-Time Team in 2000, and he was elected to the Pro Football Hall of Fame in 1979, his first year of eligibility. In 1994, the Chicago Bears retired his number (51) signifying that there would never be another number 51 for the Chicago Bears.

After football, Butkus appeared in a number of films, television shows, and was a pitchman for several products. He has also served as a sports analyst for CBS. In 2008, Butkus initiated a nationwide campaign to help eliminate anabolic steroid use by high school athletes called "I Play Clean." He's asking all athletes to take the "I Play Clean" pledge to not use performance-enhancing drugs and to eat right, train hard, and play with an attitude.

Dick has been married to his high school sweetheart, Helen, since 1963. They have three children, a daughter and two sons.

"I was born in Chicago. I was the youngest of nine kids. My father worked as an electrician at Pullman Standard, and my mother worked in the laundry.

"Being the youngest of the kids, I always looked up to my older siblings. They all participated in sports. But they weren't too interested in having me around or doing things with me. My closest brother was four years older than me and didn't want me hanging around with him. So, it was kind of frustrating to try and hang out and participate with my older brothers.

"We lived on a dead end street, and there was a park, Fernwood Park, just down the street from our house. We were always hanging out there and playing different sports. I just naturally followed my brothers to the park, because that's where they were hanging out. Even though I didn't get to participate with them a lot, they probably were a big influence on me wanting to play sports.

"I never played organized football until high school, but we played a lot of pick-up style football in the park. Each park had their own football teams that would play one another, but I was always too big or too young to qualify to play on one of the park league teams. But we had a group of guys who would play together. Usually, we would always play older kids. We always seemed to play a level up as kids, so we had to do our best to be competitive against the older kids.

"Each season at the park meant a different sport. We were in the park constantly. You wouldn't think that we would stay out there in the winter, considering the Chicago weather, but they would flood the football field and we would play games on the ice.

"The first organized sport I participated in was swimming at the local city pool. I remember there were two brothers who had played on the Olympic water polo teams who helped out there. We got introduced to water polo at a very early age. So, my first sport was being on the swim team, and my second organized sport was little league baseball.

"My parents were very supportive of our athletics. They were there for every football game. It was always our decision to play or not play a sport. Being from Lithuania, I don't know how much my parents actually understood the game, but I remember watching my brothers play football with my parents and, by the time I started playing, I suppose they understood some things about the game. My parents didn't have any input into our playing, but they were always there supporting us.

"I didn't have any particular professional role models growing up. We didn't watch much television when I was a kid, so I didn't really have much exposure to the professional players. My brothers were probably the biggest role models I had to play sports. I also used to watch a real good high school team, Bangor High School. They were pretty close to my house, and they were always winning championships at that time.

"I don't know exactly what or who motivated me to want to become a football player, but by the time I was in the fifth grade I decided that I was going to be a professional football player. I worked hard at becoming one, just like society says you should. If you work hard, you can achieve your goals. I understood that to be a professional football player you had to be tough and fierce. I was tough. I was fierce. I understood that in the fifth grade.

"As a kid, I always had to play physically. I was usually younger than the kids who were the same size as me, and I was very shy about that and didn't have too much to say when I was playing with the older kids. That's where a lot of my desire developed. I would let my actions speak louder than my words, so to speak. If I thought the other kids weren't treating me the way I thought I should be treated, I'd take it out on them on the football field.

"As far as ethical role models, I would say that my father and my brothers were probably the most influential in that category. I remember my father would moonlight at night with side jobs. Sometimes people would call him and tell him that whatever he had fixed wasn't working right. He would always go back and make sure the job was done right. He had a certain dedication and pride in his work and impressed upon me the importance of doing a job right the first time, so you didn't have to go back and do it twice.

"My father was a soft-spoken man. Maybe that was because he came over from Europe and had a lack of confidence in his English-speaking abilities. But his work ethic had a big impression on me as a kid. No matter what I was going to do, I wanted to make sure I did it the right way. When I did that, I felt good about myself, and I avoided conflicts with other people by doing the best I could.

"I think the traits I developed as a kid came more from my parents than from athletic participation. I mean it's great to be exposed to sports and learn about teamwork and other character attributes, but you have to have something in place before you can learn or develop those kinds of traits. If the foundation isn't there before you start participating athletically, you're at a disadvantage, and the values you need to succeed are more difficult to develop without the influence of the parents at home to help impart those values into you at an early age.

"But that's not to say that athletics doesn't influence your character in a big way. I had a great high school coach, Bernie O'Brien. He was a great, great man and had a tremendous influence on me and the other team members. And it wasn't just the starters on the team whom he influenced. He shared his philosophy with everybody.

"Coach O'Brien had played at Notre Dame, and I was being recruited by Notre Dame. I respected the fact that he didn't try to coerce me to sign with Notre Dame or any other school. He left that decision up to me and respected my right to make my own choice. I also remember one time I got in a little trouble, and Coach O'Brien called me in and told me that it didn't matter how good of a football player I was, if I kept on getting in trouble, I wouldn't be able to play football anywhere. He certainly helped us as football players, but I think he was as much, if not more, concerned about us as humans. He was a great guy.

"I had the success I had because I had the desire to succeed. I think that others who have the ability and don't succeed simply don't have enough desire. I doubt very much if anybody made more sacrifices than I did. I had tunnel vision and was totally focused on football. You might say I went overboard with my focus, because everything I did revolved around football.

"I swam because it wasn't football season. I played baseball just to get in shape for football. I did construction work so I could carry heavy loads. When I was twelve, I used to put straps on a broken down scooter and pull my friends around the park just to get stronger legs, and I used to push an old car up and down the street just to pack on more muscle. In Little League Baseball I played catcher just so I could have collisions at home plate. I'd run up the third base line as they were coming in and knock them down before they could slide into home base. The mothers would boo me.

"Of course, the other side of that focus is what happens when you're done with football? What do you do when you're thirty years old after you retire from football? It was very difficult for me because of the intense focus I had on football to find out what was the second best thing I might love to do with my life. Football is what I was. I loved the hitting. I was made for it, and I gave the game all I had for as long as I could. I guess my only regret is that my career was too short.

"The foundations of my attitude, values, and desire are something that primarily came from my family. I would say that the core elements of these things were probably in place by the time I was around twelve. But, like I said earlier, I had these values in place before I started playing sports. The coaches and other influences served to help mature and develop those values. But, ultimately, success was proportional to the desire I had. I wanted to be recognized as the best—no doubt about it. When they say All-Pro middle linebacker, I want them to mean Butkus!

"My advice to parents today would be to let your kids participate in any and all sports that they have an interest in. If kids are driven by parents to excel in a sport they might not even want to be playing, that's going to create a problem. The kids are going to get tired of playing and want to quit, because they aren't having fun doing it anymore. And, when you're a kid, the entire point of sports and games is to have fun.

"There are so many parents these days who want their young kids to get with the program in hopes of landing a multi-million dollar contract with a pro team. A small percentage of athletes ever go on to play college sports, an even smaller percentage go on to play professional sports. So, as parents, you have to be realistic about the prospects, and sometimes parents just need to step back and let their kids play the kinds of things that interest them. Parents certainly need to show support and enthusiasm, but they don't need to be the driving force, especially with eight- and ten-year-old kids. If kids have the skill sets and desire to move on athletically, they'll do it themselves."

* * *

Thomas J. Leonard once described two kinds of structures that we use in our lives, called push and pull structures. Push structures motivate us to act or accomplish something out of a sense of duty, consequence, or fear—something that's pushing us to complete a task. Pull structures tend to pull us forward without our having to push or be pushed to complete a task. Being inspired or having a motivating vision would be good examples of pull structures.

We all have both types of structures in our lives, and most of us have more push structures than pull structures. There's nothing wrong with push structures, but as we develop, we often find that pull structures are more sustainable and less costly in terms of the effort we expend and what we're able to accomplish. If you're building a stone church, it's just much more effective to visualize your work as an artistic endeavor that will positively impact people's lives than it is to think of your work as just another day where you have to lift all those heavy stones. The way you see things often defines the kind of structure it is.

A vision is the act of anticipating that which will or may come to be. Bill Gates had a vision about the operating systems for computers. His vision was so clear and compelling it pulled him forward to do his part in making Microsoft an ultra-successful company. Compared to a vision, goals are generally less powerful. While goals are good to have, they invariably require a number of push structures to achieve them.

Dick Butkus had a vision of being a professional football player when he was in the fifth grade. It wasn't a goal or something he thought he might like to do. It was an absolute—there was no other option in his mind. His vision pulled him through his career and kept his desire burning so bright that when you say "linebacker" today, his is the first name that pops into mind.

Chapter 4

LARRY CSONKA

Satisfaction lies in the effort, not the attainment.
Full effort is full victory.
— Mahatma Gandhi

Lawrence (Larry) Richard Csonka was born in Akron, Ohio, on December 25, 1946. One of six children, he was raised on a farm in a Hungarian family. He played high school football at Stow-Munroe Falls High School from 1960-1963.

Csonka became a running back by accident. In the last game of his high school sophomore year he was sent in as a substitute on the kick-off return team. He received the kickoff, took off running and loved the feeling he got from carrying the ball. While his coaches doubted he could be a running back, his performance in his first game as a junior proved he could be a running back.

Csonka played college football at Syracuse University from 1965 to 1967 and was named an All-American. He broke many of the school's rushing records, amassing 2,934 yards, 100-yard gains in fourteen games, and an average of 4.9 yards per carry. He was the Most Valuable Player in the East-West Shrine Game, the Hula Bowl, and the College All-Star Game. He was enshrined in the College Football Hall of Fame in 1989.

Larry was the number one pick by the Miami Dolphins in 1968, and the eighth player picked overall. By the 1970s he was one of the most feared runners in professional football, standing 6′3″ and 235 pounds. He was described as a bulldozer or battering ram. Minnesota Vikings linebacker, Jeff Siemon, said, "It's not the collision that gets you. It's what happens after you tackle him. His legs are just so strong, he keeps moving. He carries you. He's a movable weight."

Csonka was known for his toughness. He broke his nose about a dozen times throughout his career. He may be the only running back to ever receive a personal foul for unnecessary roughness while running the ball, when he knocked out safety John Pitts (Buffalo Bills) with a forearm shot that was more like a right cross punch. He was named the tenth toughest football player of all time in the 1996 NFL films production of *The NFL's 100 Toughest Players*. Monte Clark, a Dolphins coach, said, "When Csonka goes on safari, the lions roll up their windows."

Csonka and his teammate, Jim Kiick, were known as Butch Cassidy and the Sundance Kid. In 1974, Csonka, Kiick and teammate Paul Warfield signed contracts to play in the new World Football League. The three played for the Memphis Southmen, but the league folded midway through its second season.

As a free agent, Csonka joined the New York Giants in 1976. At the end of the 1978 season, Csonka's contract was up with the Giants, and he returned for a final season with the Miami Dolphins in 1979.

In his eleven-year career, Csonka carried the ball 1,891 times for 8,081 yards and sixty-four touchdowns. He was among the NFL's top-10 ranked players in rushing yards four times, rushing touchdowns five times, total touchdowns three times, and yards from the line of scrimmage once. He was All-AFC four times, All-Pro three times, and selected to play in five Pro Bowls.

Csonka played on two Super Bowl championship teams (Dolphins, Super Bowls VII, VIII) and was a part of the Dolphin's perfect season in 1972, the first team (since the AFL-NFL merger) to ever go undefeated and untied. In 1973, he was voted the MVP of Super Bowl VIII and as Super Athlete of the Year by the Professional Football Writers Association. The Miami Dolphins retired his number (39) in 2002, and he was inducted into the Professional Football Hall of Fame in 1987.

Since his retirement, Csonka became a motivational speaker, has had periodic appearances on various TV shows, and has hosted several hunting and fishing shows.

" **I** was Born in Akron, Ohio, and lived in a little town called Stow. My mom was a housewife, and my dad worked for Goodyear Tire and Rubber Company. Before the war he was a tire builder, but he had war injuries and came back and worked as the head of the tool room and was a part-time machinist. I had two older brothers, two older sisters, and one younger sister.

"We grew up in the country, and we had a lot of responsibility. We had animals and a small farm, around twenty acres, and my brothers and I all worked on large dairy farms adjacent to the place I grew up. That's something I talk about often in the motivational speaking I do, the importance of being out and working hard as a youth.

"As kids, we had very little idle time. The *idle hands* thing was definitely something that worked on us. If I had too much time on my hands, I tended to get in trouble. But trouble then had a different definition than trouble now. Trouble now takes on a whole new connotation and can be much more serious.

"In junior high and high school I think athletics were something our family really moved toward. We had a pretty athletic family because we were poor, and we worked hard, and we were strong, healthy young kids. We ate well, but we worked hard, and as a result, we had strong backs and were pretty determined. If you have to dig 200 postholes with a spade and mattock, you learn about discipline and hard work, getting blisters, and getting a job done.

"As far as a neighborhood, there wasn't one. We walked a mile on a cow path to where the school bus picked us up, and that was rain, shine, summer, winter, spring, fall, and sometimes in snow up to your knees. We didn't spend a lot of time complaining about it. It was just a fact of life, and that was the way it was. Everybody had to do it.

"The first organized sport I got involved with was little league baseball. I did pretty good at that. I was a big kid, and I was pretty quick for a larger than normal kid. The influence to play sports was a combination of things. Sports were looked upon very brightly in our house. My father liked that and so did my mother. It was somewhat of a social event when one of us was involved in something where the rest of the family could all go and watch. It created an adhesion in our family—a family camaraderie. We all pulled for each other. We would fight like cats and dogs amongst each other, but if you messed with a Csonka, you messed with all of us. I think that's a family trait that carries on today.

"My parents were supportive of athletics. But, on the other hand, I was the one who had to make it happen. I hate to sound like Abe Lincoln, but that's the way it was. I had to finish my chores and ride my bicycle about five miles to school because I stayed after school for sports. Then I had to ride the bicycle home and finish my chores. They weren't massive chores, but they were outside responsibilities. I had animals that depended on me to feed them. Dad made the point very early that the critters eat before you do. *Don't you eat until they've eaten.* That may sound real tough, but those responsibilities had to be done.

"I had to earn the time to get to play sports. I think that's a big difference in today's kids. A lot of times it would be nice if all kids had responsibilities of critters like that because you learn a lot about life with animals. You learn about life, death, and birth; you know, the whole thing is right there in front of you and sometimes graphically to the point that it's really making you think about it.

"I think every kid should have a chance to work on a big dairy farm—birthing calves and helping assist a cow with a calf and getting him cleaned up and getting him started on how to nurse. You get to be mother to these calves, and at the other end of the spectrum you see the butchering process, and everything starts to fall in line, and you realize a lot of things about life and death, and how you live your life and what sympathy and emotions mean. You get to relate that to getting along with others as well as the critters here on earth.

"Playing sports was pretty much my decision. I don't ever recall my parents being reluctant about my participation. But some sports were more prohibitive than others. Wrestling was tough because it was in the dead of winter, and we lived in a pretty inaccessible place. Sometimes it was impossible for me to get back and forth. We had only one car, and with six siblings, you kind of had to work those things out for yourself, which if you wanted to do it bad enough, you would count on friends and parents of friends to assist in giving you a ride sometimes. That was kind of a community thing. It taught me about community and taught me respect for my neighbors and the parents of my friends.

"When I was first getting into football and really liking it, I watched a fellow named Charley Tolar, a fullback from the Houston Oilers. Of course, I watched Jim Brown of the Cleveland Browns, too. I liked running the ball. That was the thing I would practice on the farm. I would run downhill in woods that had loose footing and just try to dodge the trees. There were a lot of things I did in practice on the farm that went into the athletic part. I liked to play the game for the feeling of accomplishment. I didn't really dream about being a star running back in the NFL or anything like that. It was more on the plane of junior high sports or something like that.

"I got in a lot of trouble around the fifth through the eighth grade. I got bullied around quite a bit when I was a younger kid. Being the youngest in the class and not knowing a lot about fighting, I took a lot of punishment, and it made me...well, it ticked me off. I couldn't wait to get even, and *even* wasn't good enough. I wanted to get doubly even.

"So, I became somewhat of a bully myself toward those people who had done those things to me. I over punished them. One summer I grew two or three inches and put on twenty pounds and went back to school and proceeded to thump anybody who had ever laid a hand on me—way past what was even.

"Then a fellow entered my life named Saltis. He was a junior high principal and an eighth grade science teacher. He took me aside and talked to me a lot and just spent some time with me. I think more than anyone else, he had a lot to do with me staying in athletics and realizing that, if I didn't clean up my ways, I wasn't going to be able to play. It was a reward to be able to participate in athletics, and if I were going to follow the trail that I had been following, pretty much being a little jerk, I would not be afforded that opportunity.

"When I was in the eighth grade, I got to play on the freshman football team for one game because I was getting a little bigger. I played in a game against a team that was much older, probably a JV team made up of sophomores and some juniors and seniors who couldn't make the varsity team. We lost miserably, but I played quite a game. I couldn't stand the thought of them mocking us. It just tore me up. I was walking off the field on the brink of tears, just mortally upset. I was really ticked. I viewed them as kind of bullies taking advantage of us because they were so much stronger than us.

"And Mr. Saltis walked up and put his arm around me and said, *What are you upset about?* I told him and he said, *I'm going to tell you something, Larry. You're the only football player on that field.* And that really hit home with me. That's one of the two times in my life that people have told me things that I just believed with my core.

"The other time was when I was five years old and my grandmother was watching us kids at the farm. I was mortally afraid to go down to the outhouse because the older kids had told me about the bogeyman, and it was 10:00 p.m. But I had to use the bathroom, and I had to go out. I was just beside myself. I didn't want to go out there. My grandmother picked me up. I really loved her, and anything she said was gospel to me. She picked me up and stood me up on a kitchen chair, then she whispered in my ear. She said, *I'm going to tell you something, but you have to swear to me that you'll never tell anybody else until you're grown.* I said fine. She leaned over and looked all around and whispered in my ear, She said, *Gooch* (my nickname was Gooch) *you are the bogeyman!*

"And it changed everything. Not only was the dark no longer a source of my fear; it was my friend. I could go out there and hide and scare other people out of their wits, and in the long run it probably got me in a lot of trouble. As a kid, it was like turning the light on, and I'm sure my grandmother didn't have any idea how much weight her words carried with me, but when she told me that, it just changed my life. I went from being a quivering bowl of Jell-O® in the dark, to being what everyone is afraid of in the dark. At least that's how it seemed in my five-year-old mind.

"My older brother, Joe, was seven years older than me, and I thought he was really cool because he drove cars when I was about ten and worked and bought his clothes at particular places. He was a significant role model to me. To my knowledge, he has never told an out-and-out lie in his life. He was, and is, a great influence in my life because he has such a tremendous sense of fair play, which I think he learned from my mother.

"He had a lot of values and things you need to get along in the world. He wouldn't begin to let himself be pushed around, but at the same time he afforded people opportunities to either prove themselves as a friend or a foe, without jumping to conclusions. Just watching him deal with his friends and how ethical he was about the truth had a big impact on me.

"But it's very confusing today because a kid turns on the TV—something we didn't have until I was twelve years old—and you wonder how much the TV has to do with shaping the character of kids today. I mean, by the time you're twelve, you've pretty well shaped your character. On TV, the truth means very little. You don't really know if it's real or if it's a lie. I think it confuses young people.

"My football coaches had a great influence on me as a player and as an individual. I already mentioned Coach Saltis, but in the seventh and eighth grade we had a gym teacher by the name of Carol Sloop. He was a part-time scout for pro baseball and knew a lot about that. He was a man of no nonsense. If you disturbed his gym class and got into a fight, it better be a good one or he'd make your butt black and blue for your trouble. If he walked out on to the field when you were fighting, you would start fighting extra hard to make sure it was a good fight, because if you weren't marked up by the time he got there, he'd make sure that you wore a couple of his marks. You weren't going to disturb his time.

"But he was a fair individual, too. He took an interest in my athletics and spoke to me on several occasions and encouraged me. Mr. Sloop would kind of tap you on the shoulder and say, *How you doing, slugger?* That meant he liked you. He was a man of few words, but he didn't take any BS at all, and in his class you could hear a pin drop. At the same time he had a sense of humor, and he liked all the kids, particularly the kids who were involved in athletics. He was sympathetic to the less athletic kids and never singled them out or tried to humiliate them. He tried to encourage them and get them in situations where they could perform athletically against someone more of their own caliber. That always impressed me.

"I think my character continued to develop even into pro football. Coach Shula had a tremendous affect on that. He was a strong disciplinarian, and it was almost a military-type atmosphere. There was a need to excel, not just winning, but to be the best you could be. That was his motto, and we achieved that with the undefeated season.

"Do I miss it? Yes, I do. I don't miss holding the Super Bowl trophy. I don't miss being on TV as a football player. I don't miss two-a-day practices in August. What I do miss is being in a situation when all the money is on the line, and you're down on the other team's four-yard line, and it's fourth down and one yard to go.

"That's what I miss—stepping into that huddle and looking at the faces of five offensive linemen who have been through three years of sweat and toil with me at those two-a-day practices in south Florida, who had gone through all the suffering and work, through the losses and the hard times. To step into that huddle and look at their faces and every one of them staring at me knowing I'm going to get the call, and every one of them wanting me to follow them. I miss that a lot. I dream about it.

"That's probably the greatest camaraderie I'll ever be afforded in my lifetime. Even now, as an American, when I see the news about the war, it evokes that spirit in me. I'm not saying that I'm part of the gang in Iraq, but I know the feeling those men and women feel when they step into their group looking at each other's faces, understanding the intensity of accomplishing a goal that you feel is right and just. You get a sampling of that same kind of thing in athletics.

"Many times in the course of my career I would go over with the linemen and get into their drill with them. I liked that, because then you weren't just standing around or running some little fairy pass pattern. You were over there with the men. It built a bond, and I hung out with the linemen, on and off the field. It was a microcosm of what this country is all about. All different races, different creeds, different religions were in that huddle. We were all the same in there.

"For players to be singled out because they carry the ball is BS. They start reading that stuff and start believing it and making statements like they'll play when they feel like it. They're totally out of touch with what the whole thing is about. That kind of stuff destroys what the whole idea of sports is about, and that's the danger of professional athletics in this country. It starts to poison all the kids because they start to emulate what they see in the pros. That individualism has no place on a football field. It's a team sport, and the more you make it a team sport, the more likely you are to succeed, particularly as a running back. Walter Payton—that's all I need to say, because he was the perfect example of how it should be. If we could all mimic him, it would be a great place to live, wouldn't it?

"As far as why I was able to achieve the levels I did might be summed up in a simple statement: If I rest, I rust. I just always had energy to go on. I didn't even like to sit down at the breaks because I thought I was going to get too comfortable, and I hated the feeling when I had to stand back up again. So, I kind of stayed in the game by just standing up. When you sit down and turn your back on the game, it's hard to get back in it. If you're really in it, you're in it every second of the way. That's what I sold out to. That's the way I lived.

"Everything that I ever did, that I liked, I did to excess. Some things good, some things bad. I drank a lot of Jack Daniels till I was about forty, then I quit, just that quick. That was a thing that was hurting me, so I quit. Hopefully when you're doing something that's bad for you, somewhere along the line you start to realize it's not a good thing because it's starting to mitigate some of the other things or goals you want to accomplish. So, you discipline yourself to cut that activity out. You have to have the kind of discipline that allows you to control your body and your mind in sports, and you can apply that same discipline in everyday life. You just have to know when to shut the valve off and when to throw it wide open.

"By the time I was twelve or thirteen, I probably had a lot of my value systems in place. But I think that you continue to learn values your whole life. There's a point where you have to decide whether you're going to be a good person and that you're going to stand for the truth. And when you're confronted with those kinds of decisions, no matter how humiliating it might be, you're going to do the right thing. While I'm certainly not perfect, it's a fact that what I know to be right and wrong, I learned from watching certain people I've known in my life. Throughout the course of my life, there are probably ten or twelve significant people who are responsible for shaping my values and my perception of life.

"As far as any advice I might offer to parents today, I'd say make sure you read a story to your kid every night. I wish I had. Those are times you can't get back. I had so many things going on with my professional career that I missed a lot.

"I used to take my boys fishing when they were around four and six. I would take a bucket, a lantern, and a little lab puppy out there and just lay on the bank while the kids would fish for minnows so they could take them back home and put them in our pond. They would catch the minnows and bounce them off my face because I was falling asleep. Between a wet lab puppy and the minnows hitting me in the face, it's one of the fondest memories I have of their childhood. I wish I had done that more. You don't get that back once they're grown.

"Now I get to spend a lot more time with my grandkids. I'm kind of making up for lost time with their parents. Maybe that's the great thing about living long enough to become a grandparent. You get to correct a lot of things you missed the first time around. So, take your kids fishing, but take them to a place where they'll also have a good time playing on the shore. Don't take them out in a boat and make them sit for hours trying to catch fish that may not be biting. Take them to a place on the shore, and make sure you've got a puppy along so they'll be entertained all afternoon as much as you'll be irritated. Later on you'll love to remember it."

* * *

On the field of competition there are times, magical moments, which give a participant an opportunity to tap into an elevated physical and mental state, where one is totally focused on the moment and the inward reflection is elevated to new levels. No longer are there external factors—there's no crowd, there's no pain, there's no chaos. There is only, as John Updike once wrote, "the hard blue glow of high purpose."

One might wonder why an athlete would subject him or herself to the torture of the preparation it takes to tap into higher physical and mental levels. Perhaps one answer would be that this "zone" is the one place where an athlete can experience the euphoria that goes along with having the chance to live completely in the present moment—a moment where your body and mind have achieved elevated limits of their potentials.

No doubt, Larry Csonka and his teammates had their share of magical moments that helped them achieve the first ever perfect season in professional football. But they got even more than that out of the experience. They were a part of a structure that gave them a glimpse of excellence, and because they endured and persevered, they got to take that experience with them beyond the field and apply those qualities to their lives. It's not so much the destination they arrived at as a team that becomes the most important part of their experience. Maybe it's more about who they were, what they did, and what they became along the ride that became the more defining characteristic that made them what they are today.

Chapter 5

LEN DAWSON

He who would accomplish little must sacrifice little;
he who would accomplish much must sacrifice much;
he who would attain highly must sacrifice greatly.
— *James Allen*

Leonard Ray "Len" Dawson was born in Alliance, Ohio, on June 20, 1935. He was the seventh son of a seventh son.

Dawson was recruited out of Alliance High School by Purdue Assistant Coach Hank Stram. In his three seasons at Purdue, Dawson threw for over 3,000 yards, leading the Big Ten Conference in that category each year he was at Purdue.

Dawson was drafted in the first round of the NFL Draft by the Pittsburgh Steelers in 1957. He played for the Steelers until 1959, when he was traded to the Cleveland Browns. Dawson was traded to the Dallas Texans in 1962, a move that reunited him with Texans' Head Coach, Hank Stram.

In his first season with Dallas, he led the league in touchdowns and yards per attempt and was one of *The Sporting News'* 1966 AFL All-League players. In 1963, the Texans moved to Kansas City where Dawson's abilities continued to flourish.

Dawson won four AFL passing titles, was selected as a league All-Star six times, and was the highest rated career passer in the ten-year existence of the AFL. He played in Super Bowl I, the first championship game between the AFL and NFL. He also played in Super Bowl IV, the last game played by an AFL team, and was the Most Valuable Player in that contest against the Minnesota Vikings.

43

Dawson earned Pro Bowl honors following the 1971 season and ended his career in 1975, having completed 2,136 of 3,741 passes for 28,711 yards and 239 touchdowns. He is a member of the Kansas City Chiefs Hall of Fame, and was enshrined in the Pro Football Hall of Fame in 1987.

" I was born in Alliance, Ohio, in 1945. I was one of eleven children. I was the youngest of seven boys, and I had two older sisters and two younger sisters. We were a big group.

"My dad was born in Ohio but was raised in England. My grandfather had come to the United States because there was no work in the coal mines in England at the time. When my father's mother died at childbirth, my grandfather moved my father and the children back to England. So, my dad was actually raised in England and married there and had two children. He came back to the United States to maintain his citizenship. His work background was basically as a laborer. He worked in the coal mines, pottery plants, and machine shops.

"My mother was basically a homemaker. With eleven kids, she rarely got out of the house.

"The neighborhood I grew up in was mixed with different nationalities. It was a combination of European groups, such as Italians, Germans, Polish, or Romanians. We weren't rich by any means. We were more on the poor side. Of course, we didn't really know that because everybody was in the same boat. My parents never even owned a car. If you went somewhere, you either walked, bicycled, or hitched a ride with someone.

"It wasn't really that competitive of an environment around my house, as far as my brothers were concerned. My closest brother was six years older than me, and my oldest brother was sixteen years older than me. But it was probably my brothers who had more to do with my interest in sports than anything else.

"Mostly, the older kids helped raise the younger ones. When you started school, it was one of the older kids who was in charge of you and took you to school. I just kind of tagged along with one of them. I've heard stories about me getting lost while I was following them, when one of my siblings would look around and say, *Where's Leonard?* I'd end up down at the police station, and somebody would have to come pick my up there.

"While it wasn't really competitive around my house with my brothers, there was a lot of competitive spirit with the other people I associated with. We organized our own teams and scrounged around with different merchants to kind of beg for money to buy equipment and tee shirts, which got the name of the business stenciled onto it. The parents didn't have much to do with it. We kids organized the entire thing.

"My parents didn't have any role in my athletic career. My mother was born and raised in England, and my father was raised there. Women back then really weren't involved in sports. By the time my dad was about fifteen and had completed his formal education, he went to work in the coal mines. My dad did know something about soccer, but they were a poor family and didn't have the luxury of sports.

"It was my brothers who got me involved in sports. They would take me aside and teach me the fundamentals of some of the games. I had one brother who really loved baseball, and he played in high school. He would take me to a field about three or four blocks away from our house and teach me things about baseball. He taught me how to hit, how to field properly, and other fundamentals. I really loved baseball.

"My oldest brother was very good at basketball, and he taught me the fundamentals of that game when I was in the third or fourth grade. When I started playing organized sports in grade school, I had more knowledge about the games than most kids my age.

"My brothers played a critical role in helping me gain some knowledge about the fundamentals of baseball and basketball. One brother used to run the youth leagues at the Methodist church, and I was kind of like a gym fly then. In between quarters I'd go out on the court and shoot and practice. But I remember both of my brothers stressing the importance of learning the fundamentals of the games, because they would say the better you learn the fundamentals, the better you're going to be at playing the game.

"My oldest brother was solid as a rock morally, and in every other way. I think that trickles down to the other family members. If you've got a bad apple at the top of the barrel, oftentimes that results in a lot more rotten apples. I think I was very fortunate to come from a big family. I remember getting my mouth washed out with soap by my sisters for saying something disrespectful, and the discipline frequently got handed down from an older sibling.

"But no one ever taught me the fundamentals of football as a kid until I started playing organized football. But the importance of learning the fundamentals and the rules in the other sports helped me in everything I did athletically.

"When I was about ten years old, I remember being asked to participate on a baseball team. I was just elated that somebody would ask me to play on a team. It was called the Hot Stove League in those days, and it was for kids who were thirteen or fourteen years old. So, when I was ten, I was competing with kids three or four years older than me, and I enjoyed some success with baseball. When I was about twelve years old, our team won the league championship.

"As a kid, we played whatever sport was in season. Before I got into organized football, we would play on a field we called Goat Hill, by our house. That's where all the kids would gather, and I learned a lot at a young age, because I was often younger than many of the other kids. We would organize the games, set the rules, and set the boundaries.

"Sports was our outlet as kids. We didn't have a television, but we would listen to the baseball games on the radio. Parents certainly weren't going to entertain us, because they had jobs, houses, and families to take care of. We basically gathered up and figured out ways to entertain ourselves. It might be baseball, football, hide-and-seek, or Kick the Can. Today, I wouldn't be surprised if kids asked you if Kick the Can was a video game.

"Just about everything we did had a physical dimension to it. But a lot of it had a mental component to it, too. In addition to having to figure out the rules and getting equipment and things like that, many of the games we played required strategic thinking. You had to create strategies to end up winning a King of the Hill game; you needed strategies to figure out how to get the guy out who was in between bases. You were always using your head, thinking about the best way to win. We had to think for ourselves to find ways to entertain ourselves. Sitting in front of a television or video game kind of removes that element.

"We all had chores to do around the house when I was a kid. My chore was to help my sisters do the dishes. Since the ball field was only a few blocks from our house, I developed my quickness at the dinner table so I could beat it out the back door to the ball field, leaving my sisters to do my chores.

"I also had a newspaper route when I was a kid, and there were times when that job kind of interfered with my interest in baseball, because if I hit the baseball diamond, my attention went from delivering papers to playing ball. My customers would start calling the house wanting to know where their papers were, and my sister would have to go finish my route.

"I had a lot of good coaches who had an influence on me. My high school football coach helped me a lot. While I had always been encouraged by my brothers and my parents to do the best at whatever I was doing, it was Coach Nolten who really had an impact on me as far as viewing sports as more than just something I loved to do. After my junior year in high school, the coach came up to me and told me I had the ability to get a scholarship.

"I hadn't thought that much about a scholarship, because I just loved playing, and I played everything. I loved to compete and do the best I could do at whatever I was doing. But when Coach Nolten showed that kind of confidence in me, it really rang a bell, especially since I had five of my brothers in WWII at the time. He was a great quarterback coach and taught me the fundamentals of the quarterback position that took me through college and nineteen years of professional football.

"I think the first time I ever played organized football was in the eighth grade. Back then, coaches would look around at the students to see who might look like a good football player, then ask those kids to play. I was a pretty lightweight kid, and I remember I didn't get selected to play junior high football in the seventh grade. When I did get selected, they put me at the defensive lineman position because one of my brothers had played that position. I felt like I was on roller skates at that position, because as I went forward, as soon as I met the resistance of the opposing player, I went backwards just as fast.

"Our team only had one quarterback, and the coach was looking for volunteers at that position, and my hand went up fast. I wanted out of the middle of the pit! I couldn't throw it the farthest, but I did have a little spiral on my passes. The coach said I looked more like a quarterback than a defensive lineman, so I ended up getting the second team quarterback spot.

"As luck would have it, the starting quarterback's family moved out of town that summer, and I became the starting quarterback. But we had such good teams back then that all I basically had to do was hand the ball off to the running backs.

"I didn't have much size as a kid, and I was much more competitive at baseball, which was my favorite sport. I did pretty well at basketball, too. Our basketball coach was also the baseball coach, and he had played high school sports with my oldest brothers, so he was like a family friend. He had a great deal of influence on me. He would take a little extra time and work with me because he was kind of like family.

"Coming from a poor family with eleven kids doesn't exactly set the stage for success. But I had people all around me that stressed if you were going to get anywhere in this life, you better do whatever you're doing to the best of your ability and try and get an education.

"I had several brothers who attended college on the GI bill. I had two sisters who went to college. My father had no choice about higher education, because the times he grew up in required that you go to work when you were about fifteen years old, and women in the early 1900s weren't even expected to do anything as far as education was concerned.

"But I had people all around me who were moving forward and encouraging me, and I think that one of the most significant changes in the reality I had was when my high school coach told me I had the opportunity to get a full football scholarship. That really opened my eyes to an entirely new world of opportunities.

"I had been playing sports just because that was what I really liked to do more than anything else. I didn't think beyond that. My coach explained to me the kind of opportunities I might be looking at and stressed that it would take more than just athletic skills to take advantage of my opportunities. He made me realize that I had to be able to academically qualify to take advantage of a scholarship. That opened my eyes to the importance of an education, and I went from being an average student to a much better than average student because of that realization.

"I got more focused on being organized and being prepared. I remember one of my brothers telling me that there are going to be a lot of distractions during the first year of college. He stressed to me to set some time aside to hit the books instead of cramming for an exam the night before. I had been taught to expect the best and prepare for the worst, so you don't have a major problem if the unexpected turns up. The organization and preparation were things that I applied to my life and were things that were very important in my athletic career, where you've got to be organized and prepared to be competitive and play at higher levels.

"In achieving the things I have athletically, I'd say hard work was another critical thing that contributed to my success. But, as I look back, it really wasn't hard work, because I enjoyed it. I remember seeing an old friend of mine, and we were talking about how I used to go over to Goat Hill as a kid and just throw the football around by myself. I can remember looking in a mirror and critiquing my first step back from the center, just so I could make sure I was in the right position.

And I worked on all kinds of things that other people weren't working on. I think all that goes back to being taught the importance of fundamentals at an early age.

"I had some natural ability, but somebody along the way had to teach and explain the importance of the fundamentals that enable you to take advantage of your ability. As I got older, I took great pride in the fact that, fundamentally, I knew my position. I knew what I was doing, whether it was football or any other sport. I was one of the few high school players selected for the All-State High School team in football and basketball in the same year. It wasn't just natural ability. It was a combination of that ability, what you had been taught, and how you applied that information.

"There's just so much that goes back to my older brothers and their influence on me. They would tell me to find out the best way to do something, and if you didn't know, ask someone. And don't be afraid to ask, just tell the coach that you don't understand exactly what he's talking about and ask him to explain it. It was the fundamentals and my ability to understand them and execute them that were the foundations for my success. I was a pretty accurate passer, and I took a great deal of pride in that. But I wasn't big, and I wasn't strong. It was the fundamentals that were so critical.

"As far as my value systems were concerned, those were embedded early in me. My older brothers and sisters set great examples and paved the way for me. They taught me right from wrong, and what was good and what was bad. Even though we grew up in a house with eleven kids and one bathroom, I feel very fortunate to have been raised in the environment I was raised in.

"The things I was taught, especially from my brothers, gave me more confidence and self-esteem. You know, when you're in the fourth or fifth grade and you have your peers looking to you because you have some knowledge of a game, or because you're able to hit a baseball or shoot a basketball, that does a lot to help your confidence.

"As far as any advice I would have for parents today, I'd say don't push your kids to play something that they might not even want to play. I never pushed my son, and he enjoyed playing sports. My son was growing up when I was playing for the Kansas City Chiefs, so there was a lot of pressure on him to play. I always told him don't play to please me. If you want to play and really enjoy it, then go ahead and play and try to be the best that you can be.

"Today there's so much money involved in sports that some parents are pushing their kids too hard to play a particular sport, with hopes that they'll become the next Tiger Woods. The emphasis is on the prospect of money instead of on the prospect of fun.

"The emphasis was completely different in my era, because the money wasn't there. The attitude was more like how we would like to compete against a particular team because they were really good. We would work extra hard preparing for a team like that from a purely competitive viewpoint. I remember when I was at Purdue and I got a little penny postcard that asked if I would be interested in continuing my football career after college. You would check yes or no. Basically, if you checked yes, you got put into the draft.

"Times have changed, but money has a way of changing things. Growing up, and even professionally, money wasn't the guiding force that determined if I played or not. The motivator was really the love of the game. Today, that's often not the case, and it's easy to lose sight of the many benefits that athletic participation can impart on a child."

* * *

It's easy to pick out the best players on a high school team. They're the ones running drills full speed. They're the ones paying attention to their opponents and strategizing how to get a step ahead of them. They're the ones on the sidelines who never take their mind off the game at hand. They're the ones who constantly think about how to improve their previous performance, and they're the ones who are out on the practice field running extra sprints with the struggling fat kid just to encourage him to dig deep and not quit. They're the leaders.

Just how did these kids become the leaders? Were they born that way, or was it something that they developed through their life exposures? Most experts would agree that the winning attitude leaders possess is a compilation of the previous experiences and external influences that an individual has. But it's not just the exposures and influences that define leadership. Perhaps even more critical is the self-assessment of those influences and the way those influences are perceived by an individual.

The little things in life often become big things, and when you're little, just about everything is big. That's especially true in a developmental sense. The way your Little League coach provides little tidbits of positive encouragement becomes a big thing in your view of the world and how you fit in it. The things your parents say to you, and the things you see your parents doing, become big things. All those things you see and hear, especially as a youngster, become the seeds of your perceptions and realities, and the better that the garden is tended, the better the opportunity for a bountiful crop of characteristics that provides a person with the fodder necessary to rise above average and express more of the potential that rests within them.

Imagine a sweet little six-year-old girl participating in the local soccer league. Her parents have never really spent much time playing kids games or throwing balls around with her, but the parents insist on her joining the soccer team. At the first soccer game, the little girl clearly doesn't have much skill or knowledge about the game. During a time out, both parents publicly chastise and harangue the child into tears because she isn't a pro-caliber soccer player, as you literally watch the spirit of her life quickly fade into some darker realm far removed from the intended motive of adding a fun, productive activity to her life.

Albert Einstein once said, "The tragedy of life is what dies in the hearts of men while they live." Outside circumstances—parents, teachers, coaches, peers—can build or destroy. Words and actions can burn the heart in a pouring rain, or they can build the heart in the midst of enormous adversity. On that fateful day, for that little innocent girl, something died in her heart, and she will tragically carry those scars to remind her wherever she goes.

Conversely, another little kid on the field, not unlike Len Dawson, comes up to his parents, and they're telling him what a great job he's doing, even though he's no more skilled than the little girl. "You're doing great out there, buddy. Are you having fun? Do your best!" are the things the little boy hears. And he keeps hearing those kinds of things every day. His heart grows fuller and his estimations of possibilities are limitless, while he learns how hard work produces positive rewards in life.

Len Dawson had a wonderful set of outside circumstances surrounding him. His siblings, his parents, his coaches, and his peers didn't tear him down. They all supported him and provided him with the tools necessary to build his confidence, so he could imbue that confidence on others around him. That's really the greatest gift Len Dawson ever had: The chance to grow up in an environment that nurtured his heart, opening the doors of limitless possibilities. Without that, chances are that he would never have accomplished what he did as a professional football player or as an honorable man.

Chapter 6

DAN DIERDORF

Act the part and you will become the part.
— William James

Daniel Lee Dierdorf was born in Canton, Ohio, on June 29, 1949. He attended Glenwood High School (now Glenoak High School) in Canton, then the University of Michigan, before being drafted by the St. Louis Cardinals in the 1971 NFL Draft.

At the University of Michigan, Dierdorf was a consensus All-American in 1970 and assisted his team to a 25-6 record in his three years as a starter. He made all-conference in 1969, the year the Wolverines won the Big-Ten championship, and was chosen for the East-West Shrine Game and Hula Bowl in 1970. He was selected for the 1971 College All-Star Game and in 2000 was inducted into the College Football Hall of Fame.

Dierdorf was drafted by the NFL in 1971 in the second round and played thirteen seasons as a St. Louis Cardinal. He began his professional football career as a guard and left tackle before settling in as a starter at right tackle. He was named to the Pro Bowl six times and was selected as an All-Pro for four consecutive seasons beginning in 1975. He was named the NFC Offensive Lineman of the year by his peers in 1976, 1977, and 1978. He was enshrined in the Pro Football Hall of Fame in 1996.

After his retirement from the NFL, Dierdorf went on to become a sports announcer and has worked with ABC and CBS as a color commentator. He resides in St. Louis and is the co-proprietor of Dierdorf's and Hart's Steakhouse.

"I was born in Canton, Ohio, and grew up there. I have two older brothers who are considerably older than me, eight and ten years older. Actually, when I was going through junior high school, I was basically home alone with my mom and dad. In some respects, it was like being an only child once I hit eight years old.

"My mother was a housewife, and my father worked at the Hoover Company, which is the company that makes vacuum cleaners. He worked there all his life.

"I lived in the same house until I went to college and I grew up in an idyllic neighborhood. I went to elementary school two blocks away, and I would always meet my friends there to play baseball and other things. My wife describes my childhood neighborhood as a *Leave It To Beaver* kind of neighborhood, and I was *Beaver!* It was a very safe, very stable, old-fashioned kind of environment.

"My oldest brother played college football at a small school in Cleveland, Ohio. At the time, it was called the Case Institute of Technology. There wasn't a competitive atmosphere between my brothers and me, because they were so much older. I was never doing anything that they were doing. When my closest brother was in high school, I was only seven or eight years old, so we never really competed in anything.

"The first organized sport I played was baseball. I was about nine or ten. I wasn't a small child, so when you've got some size, I think everybody just expects you to play sports. So, I started out with baseball. I wasn't a bad player, so long as the only thing I had to do was play defensive baseball. I was a good catcher, and I loved to play, but I could not hit the ball. I thought the signal to swing was when the ball hit the catcher's mitt! I didn't exactly get that old bat working through the wheelhouse, if you know what I mean.

"As far as my parents pushing me to play sports, they were actually the most low-key parents that anybody could ever have. While they certainly enjoyed my participation in sports and went to every game I played at any level, they never pushed me to participate. They never made me feel like it was something I had to do to please them. It was completely my choice. I truly believe that if I had chosen not to play sports, it would have been just fine with my parents. I didn't get any magic advice or encouragement from them, just unconditional support. You could not have been less obtrusive than my parents when it came to actually prodding or pushing me to do something related to sports.

"My mother would always make me the same meal before a game. My mother and father were members of the booster club, and they sat in the same section with all their other friends and parents of my teammates. From a community standpoint, they were just a couple of ducks in the pond like everyone else. But my dad never played football, so it wasn't like he had me out in the back yard helping me run drills to improve my game. And if I had a bad game, it's not like my dad made me go out and hit the blocking sled. He would just give me a pat on the back and say, *You'll do better, you'll get better.*

"My father was one of my significant ethical role models. He didn't really assert himself in terms of telling me that he wanted me to do this or that. Wisely, he always set the stage for me to come and talk to him about what I thought he wanted. That was a very smart way of doing business. My dad was a wise man in that respect. He never made me feel like he was making me do something, but he was always available to talk to. It's surprising how often I went to him to ask him things. He was a smart guy who got it done, and there was probably some psychological trickery involved there.

"I didn't start playing football until I was in the seventh grade. I didn't play Little League football because I didn't have any interest in it, and, of course, my parents never pushed me to play. As far as anyone who had a big influence on me to play, I don't know that there was anyone in particular who would fill that role. I was a big kid, and I just gravitated toward playing football. It seemed like the natural thing to do. I did love the Cleveland Browns. Cleveland was only about fifty miles from where I grew up, and Cleveland, with great players like Jim Brown, was a great team back in the sixties. And growing up in Canton, where the Pro Football Hall of Fame is located and where high school football is king, probably had some influence on my decision to play football.

"I was always a big kid, but I didn't have the coordination or aggressive attitude you needed to play football when I was younger. It seemed like I had two left feet, and my physical coordination didn't come together for me until I was eighteen or nineteen years old. So, even though I was playing the game, I wasn't all that good. I was getting by because I was bigger than everybody else. In the seventh and eighth grade I was just no good at all. My mother told me once that one of the coaches had told her, *I don't think he's ever going to be any good because nothing makes him mad. He's just the original I'm glad to be here guy.* I didn't even letter on the football team when I was a sophomore in high school. I was on the team—I just didn't get to play very much.

"It was after my junior year in high school when I realized that football might give me the opportunity to get an athletic scholarship. I remember thinking that if I had a good senior year, I might generate some interest. We were from a modest family, and my mom and dad would have found the money to send me to a local college, but I certainly would never have had the opportunities I've had if it were not for getting a college scholarship. I had never considered the possibility of a scholarship before then.

"The recruiting process back then was a little different than it is now. You didn't have websites or ESPN. It was all personal back then, and by today's standards, very slow-paced. After my senior year, I started getting letters and calls from coaches wanting me to come visit their campus. That was awfully exciting. I was a wide-eyed, pretty naïve kid when I went to visit a few colleges.

"As I look back, my high school football coach was really the guy who taught me that you have to be a man to play the game of football. He had played offensive line in college at Ohio State, and he was a tough guy. He was very demanding, and we had a good high school football team. I think that's because of how well we prepared, but it was also because all of the players were so afraid of him that we didn't want to lose because nobody wanted to see what kind of reaction the coach might have.

"I look back on that as my coach really doing me a favor, because he was the guy who taught me that football is not an easy business. Playing football is not for everybody. It's only for someone who's willing to set aside the easy route and work hard. You get knocked down, and you've got to get back up. He's the guy who got the point across that Mr. Congeniality never wins football games.

"My high school coach also taught me that football is a team game. If you participate in a team sport, someone gets the point across to you for the first time that you have to do your part for the betterment of the team. You have to hold up your end of the bargain or everybody fails. My high school coach did a wonderful job of that.

"As far as why I went on to be a success, and others who might have been stronger and faster than me didn't, I'd say the biggest reason was that it mattered to me more than anything else. At some point, I reached a point in my life where the fear of failing was the biggest motivator in my life. The mere thought of failing tortured me.

"I don't know exactly why or what made me feel that way. I think, ultimately, that it was something inside of me, but my environment certainly had something to do with it, too. I was never exposed to bad coaching. I was never exposed to meddling parents. I was never exposed to the actions of others who could have soured my athletic experience. Basically, I was allowed not to be distracted in finding out what I had inside of me.

"And that's all I think that any of us can ask for, an uncluttered path to try to find out what you really have inside. In the end, that's all that really matters. No one can do it for you. No one can flip your switch, other than yourself. What others can do is hinder you. They can throw roadblocks in your path. They can somehow sour you on the experience. But I was fortunate in the sense that I was only exposed to positives. I always received support, and I was able to find out that what I had, in God-given skills and in what I had inside of me that finally blossomed, was enough.

"I don't look back on anything that happened in my sporting life throughout high school as a negative. It was all a positive learning experience. Not that I didn't lose games or play poorly or get knocked flat on my butt. I just don't look at any of those things as having been destructive experiences.

"I think that by the time a kid is around ten or twelve years old that their value systems are basically in place. I know that was true for me. I'd been raised in such a way, and exposed to a certain set of guidelines from my parents, that everything beyond that age, as far as values go, was just an adjustment to my core values. As a father of four kids, that's been my experience.

"As far as what was important for me, I look back at the support that I got. I was proud of the fact that my mom and dad attended thirty-one of the thirty-three games I played in college. They drove to all of them and a lot of times didn't have the money to stay in a hotel, so they would leave at four in the morning and get back home at two in the morning. That kind of unconditional support, and not wanting to be the center of attention, was a real gift. I'll appreciate that until the day I die. And that's what I would encourage parents to do today. Give your kids the support they need, but give them enough room to find out what's inside of them."

* * *

There is much truth in the old cliché, "You get what you pay for." And this cliché is especially applicable when you consider your attention as the currency you pay, because it's your attention, your focus, which delivers the dividends that define your life.

We're all born with the inborn ability to focus our attention, and we do exactly that. Some people create their focal points in the gray, dreary clouds. Some folks find brighter dispositions in clear, blue skies. Everything in life has a price you pay for it, and the attention you pay toward one thing or another ultimately determines the value of what you get in return for your attention, good or bad.

The person who achieves elite status, such as a professional football player, a successful businessperson, or even a successful student, exhibits an extraordinary ability to direct his or her attention toward a desired outcome. They develop success patterns that tend to overcome the various forms of inevitable resistance that all of us meet at some point along the way.

Getting from point A to point B is a simple journey, albeit a journey often fraught with unknown challenges. Maintaining your focus to your destination is critical, as is your willingness to find the joy within the struggles before you, for when a thing matters most to you, and you're willing to do whatever is necessary to achieve your goal, then not only are you able to find celebration in the achievement of a goal, you're also able to find celebration in the struggle.

Chapter 7

MIKE DITKA

*I did the best I could. I did the best I knew how. I mean
to keep on doing it that way right up to the very end. If
the end brings me out all right, what's said against me
will not matter. But, if the end brings me out wrong, ten
angels swearing I was right will make no difference.*
— ***Abraham Lincoln***

Mike Ditka was born October 18, 1939, in Carnegie, Pennsylvania, and grew up in nearby Aliquippa, Pennsylvania. Mike was the oldest of four children, two brothers and one sister. Ditka was a three-sports star at Aliquippa High School and was recruited by Notre Dame, Penn State, and the University of Pittsburgh. Ditka played at Pitt from 1958-1960, where he was also a member of the Sigma Chi Fraternity. He started all three seasons at Pitt and is considered by most to be one of the best college tight ends to ever play. He led the team in receptions in all three seasons and was a first-team selection on the College Football All-American Team during his senior year. He was enshrined in the College Football Hall of Fame in 1986.

Ditka was the fifth overall pick in the 1961 NFL Draft when the Chicago Bears drafted him. He made an impact in his first year with fifty-six receptions and introduced a new dimension for the tight end position, which had previously been a position mainly dedicated for blocking. His early success earned him Rookie of the Year honors. For the next five years he continued playing for the Bears, earning a Pro Bowl trip each season. He also played on the 1963 championship team for the Bears. Ditka was traded to the Philadelphia Eagles in

1967 and spent two years with that club, before being traded again to the Dallas Cowboys in 1969, where he spent four years and contributed to the Cowboys win over Miami in Super Bowl VI.

Ditka amassed 427 career receptions for 5,812 yards and forty-three touchdowns. That, and his fearsome blocking, earned him the honor of being the first tight end to ever be inducted into the Pro Football Hall of Fame in 1988. In 1999, he was ranked number 90 on *The Sporting News'* list of the 100 Greatest Football Players.

Ditka retired after the 1972 season and was immediately hired as an assistant coach by Tom Landry, the Cowboys' head coach. He spent nine years as an assistant coach with the Cowboys, and they made the playoffs eight times, won six division titles, and three NFC Championships.

In 1982, Ditka was hired as the Chicago Bears head coach to help reverse the poor performance of the Bears since the retirement of the famed head coach, George Halas. Ditka led the Bears to six NFC Central titles and three trips to the NFC Championship Game. His coaching career hit its pinnacle in the 1986 victory over New England in Super Bowl XX. Many people consider the 1985 Bears defense as one of the best to ever play. The Associated Press, *The Sporting News,* and *Pro Football Weekly* awarded Coach of the Year honors to Ditka in 1985 and 1988. He concluded his relationship with the Bears after the 1992 season, and in 1997 returned to coach the New Orleans Saints for three years.

Ditka has served as a television sports commentator and analyst on several shows, hosted numerous radio shows, and appeared in several television shows, movies, and commercials. He's the owner of a chain of restaurants that bear his name, a partner in two hotel resorts in the Orlando area, owner of the Arena Football Team, the Chicago Rush, and an advocate to help raise money for former NFL players in need of assistance and medical care.

66 I was born in Carnegie, Pennsylvania, and grew up in Aliquippa. I've got two brothers and a sister, and I was the oldest of the bunch. My dad worked for a steel mill or worked for

a railroad that served the steel mill. Just about every family where I grew up had a similar story. It was a steel mill town, and everything revolved around that. Everybody had the same kinds of things, and there wasn't a whole lot more going on around there.

"One of my brothers was one year younger than me, and we were pretty competitive. We played hard, and we participated in the same sports. We played baseball, basketball, and football. So, naturally there was some competition. As I think back about it, it probably brought us closer as brothers, and we're still good friends today.

"The neighborhood I grew up in was basically a government housing project. My mom still lives there. She doesn't want to move out. There were six houses on each block, and we had a three bedroom, which was about as big as it got. When my sister came along, my brother and I had to share a bed. That was in Aliquippa, and I remember attending first grade there, so I lived there the whole time I was growing up.

"The first organized sport I played was baseball. I was about eleven or twelve years old then. We also had a Catholic football league, and I played football in the seventh and eighth grades. We played the other Catholic schools, but that league ended after the eighth grade, and we went on to public schools then.

"My parents encouraged me, and they were tremendously supportive. My dad also kept an eye on me because I had a temper. He didn't want me to get out of line, and if I did, he put me back in line in a hurry. I don't always recall seeing him at my games, but I think he made most, if not all, of the games, especially the baseball games. He must have been at most of the games, because I remember that he seemed to know everything about the games I played in.

"I don't remember my parents telling me to play this or that, or not to play. Back in those days it was always our choice if we wanted to play something. And we played just about everything. That kept us active and kept us out of trouble. Playing sports was just what we did as kids, and we were playing something all of the time.

"I played a lot of baseball as a kid. I even had a chance to sign with some teams and play professionally. The great St. Louis Cardinal,

Stan "The Man" Musial, was my hero. I thought he was the greatest and just loved him because he was from Pennsylvania, he was Polish, and he was one of the greatest hitters ever. I remember I was just a young kid when he became my hero.

"There were a lot of people who had an influence on me as far as my character is concerned. If I could only pick one specific moral role model, that would have to be my mom. But a lot of people had an impact on me, and what I am is more a combination of all of their influence.

"My high school coach was a terrific guy and a great role model. He was a very religious man, really knew the game of football, and brought championship teams to Aliquippa. I got to play on one of those teams.

"I wanted to quit playing football in high school to concentrate on baseball. I was small at the time, and when I started playing high school football as a sophomore, I was just another one of the young guys who were counted as fodder for the varsity team. The varsity players ran over us every day at practice and just about killed us. I was only about 130 pounds as a sophomore, and I wasn't too crazy about the slaughter I had to endure every day at practice. But our coach told me I'd gain some weight and encouraged me to come back out the next year. He encouraged me, taught me how to block, and I turned into a pretty good high school player as a result of his encouragement and instruction.

"The main thing our high school coach communicated was to play hard and know your assignment. I think the best advice I got from him was, *You've got to beat the guy you're playing against every time. You've got to make his all-opponent list. If you do that, you're going to win the majority of the battles.*

"The baseball coaches I had as a kid had a lot to do with the development of my character, too. So did the priests and nuns who taught me in school. They all helped mold my character. They helped me understand right from wrong and the importance of doing the things that were right. There were a lot of people who had an impact on who I am.

"I understand that a lot of kids don't agree with what their teachers and parents are telling them, and I tell them that, in reality, ninety-nine percent of what they're being told, they're being told for their own benefit. Sometimes that's a little hard to understand in high school because you think you know a lot more than you really do, until you get older and find out how little you really did know. I was fortunate to have all the good influences I had. That was nice.

"I think you become a product of your exposure. I think my desire to win was something that I learned along the way. I think that the discipline I have in my life is something that I learned. I can remember being aware of those kinds of things as a kid, and I worked hard at accomplishing them, and I really understood the work ethic thing. I figured if I was going to be able to do what I wanted to do, I was going to have to be better at certain things than others were. That was especially true when I was in high school, because I wasn't very big in the beginning. Even though I put on about fifty pounds by the time I graduated high school, and another forty by the time I went to college, without the drive I had developed, I doubt I would have accomplished what I did.

"There were many guys who probably had more talent than me. Hard work, effort, discipline, pride, and desire enabled me to accomplish more than others who didn't have the degree of commitment that I had. But all those traits are really the same thing. It all comes down to attitude. You've got a certain attitude about a certain aspect of character, and you either maximize that attitude, or you don't. I always had a certain idea about what I wanted to do, and if I was going to do it, I wanted to be as good as I could be at it. Not necessarily the best, but as good as I could be myself. I wanted to maximize my potential, so that's what I did with my football career, and that's what I still do.

"As far as developing your core values at a certain age, that's hard to really say. Maybe you get your basic values around twelve years old, but I think my values were developing more in high school than in grade school. By the time I got to high school I had a clearer idea of certain things that I wanted to accomplish. First, I just wanted to make the team. Then I got bigger and wanted to be a starter on the team. Then I had some success, and I wanted to go on to college.

"While I may have had all my core values in place by the time I was in the seventh or eighth grade, I was more aware of wanting to accomplish certain things. Perhaps that sense of accomplishment was a primary motivator to help me exhibit positive values, because in order to accomplish those things, one needs to have a certain set of values in place to realize those accomplishments.

"I loved playing sports. I played because I enjoyed it. It was what I lived for. Practice didn't even bother me. I loved to practice, too. It was like that when I was a kid, and all through high school and college. And even in pro-ball I don't ever remember playing not being fun for me. I never got to the point where I said I wish I wasn't doing this anymore. I did get to the point where I understood that my body and my skills weren't as good as they once were, and I was realistic about that. I put a lot of effort and time into building my career, and I didn't want to tear those things down by trying to continue my playing career too long, so that's when I retired.

"Being the oldest kid in our family, there was a certain amount of accountability that I had. Today, I don't think that's a predominant attitude in society. When I got out of line, my dad whipped my tail. Period. He did it the old fashioned way. I was the oldest, and the example for the other kids was set through me. The other kids never got touched, and it took me a long time to understand why I was always the one on the receiving end of his discipline.

"My dad was a Marine, and I didn't even meet him until I was two years old. He raised me a certain way, and sometimes I wondered if he really loved me. But as I got older I began to understand why people do certain things, and I came to understand that he did love me. He was tough on me because he wanted me to have more than he had. He didn't want me to have to go work in a mill like he did. He wanted my life to be better. He expected me to toe the line and do the right things so I could have the opportunities that he hoped

I would have. If I got out of line, he whipped my tail. I'm not embarrassed to say that, and he wouldn't be embarrassed to hear it.

"As far as any advice I'd have for parents today, I would say that parents are foolish to push their kids into a sport that they don't want to play. As a parent, you just can't force a kid to play a sport and expect it to be a good experience if the kid doesn't want to be out there in the first place. The only thing I ever told my four kids was, if you're gong to do something, work at it and do as good a job as you can. If you're going to go out there and waste your time, don't even do it.

"I watched my own kids play sports, and I really enjoyed watching them. It was fun for them, and it was fun for me, and I encouraged them whenever I could. But you can't push them into it. Parents can't live their lives through their kids' lives. It's great if your kids have a good athletic experience, and they get to experience the great pride and satisfaction of that experience. But, if they don't have that experience, for whatever reason, they simply don't. It's not the end of the world. There are so many other opportunities for kids, it just doesn't make sense to push them into something that they don't want to do. That rarely turns out to be a positive experience."

* * *

In his Pro-Football Hall of Fame enshrinement, Mike Ditka ended his speech with these words: "In life, many men have talent. But talent itself is no accomplishment. Excellence in football and excellence in life is bred when men recognize their opportunities and pursue them with a passion."

Those few words offer an accurate, two-part description of what is required for success. First, you must be able to recognize your opportunity. Second, you must pursue that opportunity with passion. Throughout society, in any given field of endeavor, those who attain exemplary success exhibit a compelling emotion that's attached to the activity they're pursuing.

This compelling emotion, or passion, enables a person to approach a task in a certain, deliberate way. The authors of *The Making of an Expert* describe it as "deliberate practice—practice that concentrates on tasks beyond your current level of competence and comfort." They also add that, "The journey to truly superior performance is neither for the faint of heart nor for the impatient. The development of genuine expertise requires struggle, sacrifice, and honest, often painful self-assessment. There are no shortcuts."

You can bet that Mike Ditka was more interested in advancing his skills than simply reaching a certain level and staying there. That's a common characteristic of all super achievers. They show up for practice with the intention of doing whatever they do better than they did before. And they do that day after day with a passion to express as much of their potential as they possibly can.

Chapter 8

TONY DORSETT

Man is so made that when anything fires his soul,
impossibilities vanish.
— *Jean De La Fontaine*

nthony Drew Dorsett was born April 7, 1954, in the Pittsburgh suburb of Rochester, Pennsylvania. He lived in Hopewell Township, Pennsylvania. He was a star running back at Hopewell High School and at the University of Pittsburgh. During his college career, the University of Pittsburgh captured a national title in 1976, the same year that Tony won the Heisman Trophy. He is considered one of the greatest collegiate running backs of all time.

The Dallas Cowboys drafted Tony Dorsett in 1977. He was the second pick in the first round. His stellar career in Dallas ended in 1987, and he finished his professional career with the Denver Broncos in 1988, ironically the team that Dallas had beaten in Super Bowl XII. Dorsett also appeared in Super Bowl XIII, against the Pittsburgh Steelers, who won the game 35-31.

Dorsett appeared in four Pro Bowls and was inducted into the Pro Football Hall of Fame, the College Football Hall of Fame, and the Texas Ring of Honor in 1994. He holds the record for the longest run from scrimmage (ninety-nine yards) in the NFL and is the only player in history to have won a collegiate national championship, a Heisman Trophy, a place in the Collegiate Hall of Fame, a Super Bowl championship, and a place in the Pro Football Hall of Fame.

During his career, he amassed 12,739 yards and seventy-seven touchdowns and is ranked number 53 on *The Sporting News'* list of the 100 Greatest Football Players. His son, Anthony Dorsett, played defensive back in the NFL from 1996 to 2003 and made two Super Bowl appearances.

Tony Dorsett willingly gives back to communities in both Texas and Pennsylvania. Charities he has supported include the American Heart Association, United Negro College Fund, Special Olympics, Make a Wish Foundation, and The McGuire Memorial Foundation, among others.

" **I** was born in Rochester, Pennsylvania, and grew up in Hopewell Township, Pennsylvania. I'm the sixth of seven siblings. I have an older sister, four older brothers, and a younger sister. I come from a very close-knit family. Rochester was a steel mill town, and my dad was a steel worker. My mom was a homemaker.

"I grew up in what they call the projects and spent my childhood right there on Mt. Vernon Drive. But it wasn't like we were poor, or at least I didn't know we were. I had pretty much everything I wanted. I dressed well, and mom and dad gave us just about everything we wanted as kids. I was one of the best-dressed kids in high school.

"My four older brothers were exceptional athletes, and they were my role models. I wanted to be like my brothers, and that's how I got involved in sports. Unfortunately, none of them went on to college. They pretty much got caught up in the small-town mentality and got married or went into the military. My parents or my older brothers never pushed me into sports. It was just that I wanted to be like my brothers, so I gravitated to sports.

"When I was a kid I played in the Pop Warner league. I couldn't play in the local Hopewell Pop Warner league because I was too small. My friend and I put rocks in our pockets to try and make the weight limit in Hopewell, but we were still too light. I ended up playing on the Aliquippa Pop Warner team. My brother closest in age to me played on a different team, so I never really wanted to play, and I didn't get to play that much anyway. I would drag my uniform home in the dirt just to make it look like I played.

"Basketball was the first real organized sport I played, in the seventh grade. I spent a lot of time playing sports on the playground and in the streets. That's where some of my football moves came from. You know, once you get tackled and hit the curb a time or two, you learn to avoid the object that's making you fall!

"My mom and dad didn't have much of a role in my athletic career. In fact, they never thought I was going to be an athlete. My mom nicknamed me *turtle* because I moved around pretty slow. Mom never thought I would turn out to be an athlete because I was never in a hurry. I always took my time and moved around slow. I still do that today. My mom was real surprised to see how fast I really was.

"My parents never encouraged me to get involved in sports, especially since I was pretty small. But, after junior high, and especially during high school, my mom and dad were at every game I ever played. They were a big inspiration to me.

"While my folks didn't give me much athletic advice or encouragement, my dad had a philosophy that, if you started something, you had to finish it. He believed that what you put into something determined what you got back out of it. My dad was a hard working guy in the steel mill.

"I'll never forget him telling me about the mill and how it wasn't a place I wanted to be. He would tell me that, if you got a job at the mill, there was no guarantee that you would come back out. You might be missing an arm, a leg, an eye, or something else. It was good money, but it was hard work. It was dangerous work. He would encourage me to try and do something through my education or my sports so I wouldn't have to work in the steel mill. Western Pennsylvania is blue-collar territory. That's where I got my work ethic.

"Playing sports was always my decision. My parents never force-fed me sports. That's how I raised my son, Anthony, too. To make a kid play and do something they don't want to do isn't a good thing. Of course, there was one time I wish I had gotten a little pressure to play. When I was a senior in high school and had decided to go to the University of Pittsburgh on a scholarship, I decided not to go out for my senior year of basketball. I didn't get any pressure from anybody.

I had stupid thoughts like I might get hurt or something like that. I didn't have the courage to go up to the coach and ask him if he would let me come out for the team. To this day, I regret not doing that.

"My idol as a kid, athletically, was Muhammad Ali. My father couldn't understand why I liked that man so much. My mother said he talked too much. I would tell her maybe so, but he can back it up!

"My moral role model is my mom. She was a strong lady, able to keep things in perspective as far as relationships with our dad and relationships with the kids and other family members outside of the immediate family. She didn't let too much distract her from her common goal, which was, of course, to take care of the kids and let them grow up to be decent citizens. I'd say my core value systems were in place by the time I was around twelve. I think that was about the age I started to hone in on those values and worked on them to become better at what I was trying to do.

"My high school coach, Coach Ross, was the coach whom I guess you could say really got it all started for me, to some degree. I was playing and starting as a defensive specialist, mostly because I was so small. One day Coach Ross said something about how all my older brothers were pretty good running backs and that he wanted to try me at that position. Pretty much, the rest is history from there. Things just snowballed, and I got better and better as the years went by. If it hadn't been for that, there's no saying where I might be today.

"Sports were mostly fun for me in high school. When I started getting recruited by colleges, I understood there was an opportunity for me to get an education, so the stakes were raised some, and it became a little more serious.

"When I got to the University of Pittsburgh, I could see the big picture a lot better, especially having gotten votes for the Heisman trophy as a freshman at Pitt. It was like, Wow, what's this all about? I realized that I could have an opportunity to play professional ball. But I always had detractors, too. I was always told I was too small. Coming from high school to college, I was told I was too small to be a major college running back.

"When I visited Notre Dame, the word was out that I was just a skinny little kid from Pennsylvania who would probably never make it as a major college running back. That was one of the reasons I ended up setting a career rushing record against Notre Dame, a NCAA record. Every time we played Notre Dame, I thought about that, and I was pretty motivated to play.

"Negative comments about me made me want to prove I could do what people said I couldn't. I used a negative and turned it in to a positive for myself. A couple of my brothers ended up getting in trouble when I was in high school, and some people said that I was going to end up like them, doing this or that, and getting into trouble.

"I'll never forget the day we were out on the streets of Mt. Vernon Drive when Jarret Durham said something to me that really hit a nerve. Jarret was from a rival high school and went on to play basketball at Duquesne University. He told me that I couldn't even play the game, and that I was going to be the sorriest Dorsett of them all. That just encouraged me, and I thought, I'm going to prove this guy wrong. That helped motivate me to work harder and become a better athlete.

"I had the inner drive to prove my ability, and I had a hard-core work ethic. I believe you get out of it what you put into it. In high school I ran eight miles in the morning and eight miles in the evening. I've always believed that I was going to be better, if I put in the time and effort, than the guy who was going to rest on his laurels.

"I'll never forget when I was at Pitt and one of my teammates said, *You're Tony Dorsett. Why are you practicing every day? You don't have to do this, man. Coach is not going to do anything to you.* My response to that was, I got mine, and I'm going to do it my way. When you get yours, you do it your way. I was never a guy who said I was any better than the next guy. But I believed, to stay on top, you had to work and practice hard to improve and hone your skills. I worked as hard or harder than anyone on the field. I don't think you'll ever find a coach who will tell you anything different.

"I had a lot of success in professional football. But I can't say that

I was ever totally satisfied with my performance. I don't think many athletes are. You always feel like you could have done just a little better. If you ever get to the point where you're totally satisfied with your performance, I think you're fooling yourself.

"On the other hand, as I looked at films after a game, there were plays where I couldn't believe I was doing the things I was doing. I think a lot of those plays had to do with the way I visualized the game. I used to take my game plan and I'd go through every play and visualize the play and try and figure out what my reaction would be…if this didn't happen, what would I do, if somebody misses a block, what would my next move be? You kind of mentally prepared yourself to react to different situations, then, when they happened, you instinctively reacted. You had already been through it in your mind, and when the situation came up, you were better prepared to react to it.

"You can visualize anything. Visualize your schoolwork and see yourself getting good grades, your athletic performance, your relationships, etc. The mind is a powerful device, and visualization is a powerful technique.

"Sports need to be a natural occurrence for kids. Parents can't force-feed sports to their children. If they want to play sports, that's fine. If not, then parents need to encourage their kids in whatever they want to do.

"I think there are two basic rules a parent should lay down with their kids in regard to whatever the kids want to pursue. First, if they start something, they must finish it. Second, they have to give it their best effort. The most important thing, athletically or otherwise, is to be encouraging to your kids. Sports are fun. It's fun in the little leagues, junior high school, high school, and college.

"There's a lot of pressure that comes along with professional sports, pressure that can make or break a person. There are a lot of lessons and things a child can learn from sports. Parents need to understand that sports, especially for younger children, is about learning how to play together, camaraderie, teamwork, creating friends, and having fun. It's not all about winning.

"It's very discouraging for a kid to have his or her parents place so much emphasis on winning. Kids don't need that kind of pressure, and that's one of the best ways of forcing them to not want to participate. Just let them play what they want. Encourage them. Let them have fun.

"Parents need to understand that you can't win every time, and that when you lose, you need to be a good sport. If your only standard is winning, when kids lose, they get all these bad feelings and start retreating into a shell. They're just kids; it's just a game.

"Maybe when they lose, it's better to encourage their effort and remind them that they're healthy and able to have the opportunity to do these things. We take so much for granted in life.

"I have a charity called the McGuire Memorial Foundation. It's a home for severely handicapped children. These are kids who can't walk or talk, or are all messed up because their parents left some prescription drugs out on the counter. When you see this kind of thing, you realize that we've got a lot to be thankful for. Let your kids enjoy their childhood; let them do their thing as long as it's not harmful to them. Get them away from the TVs and the computers, and get them active in something. But don't pressure them. Don't make them feel that they have to win at all costs. Just let them know that if they gave their best effort, that's enough."

* * *

Henry Ford once said, "If you think you can do a thing or can't do a thing, you're right." Whatever you see as your limits of possibility are the limits of what you can attain. Some have the ability to visualize extraordinary possibilities, even though they may not have eyes that see. Others, even with the eyesight of an eagle, can have the vision of a clam and miss the opportunities that lie directly in front of them.

Given comparable physical abilities, the individual who achieves higher goals is the person who visualizes the desired outcome. This person sees, does, and becomes that which he sees. That's the real difference between the two types—the *think I cans* and the *think I can'ts*. The *think I cans* see what they want, and have the desire and will to persist and make intelligent decisions on their way to achieving their goal. The *think I can'ts* never get the right image affixed in their mind.

In the case of the little kid, Tony Dorsett, from Mt. Vernon Drive in Pittsburgh, Pennsylvania, he could see, he would do, and he did become one of the greatest running backs in professional football. That just happened to be the dream he kept in his mind, and he turned that dream into reality.

Chapter 9

FRANCO HARRIS

Unless a man undertakes more than he possibly can do,
he will never do all that he can.
— **Henry Drummond**

F ranco Harris was born in Fort Dix, New Jersey, on March 7, 1950, to parents Cad and Gina Harris. Harris attended high school at Rancocas Valley Regional in Mt. Holly, New Jersey, where he became a High School All-American. In 1969, he attended Penn State University on a football scholarship. At Penn State, Harris rushed for 2,002 yards and twenty-four touchdowns, and played in the 1970 Orange Bowl, the 1972 Cotton Bowl, Senior Bowl, and College All-Star Game.

In 1973 Harris was drafted in the first round (thirteenth overall selection) by the Pittsburgh Steelers. He played thirteen seasons (twelve with the Steelers and one with Seattle) and became one of Pittsburgh's most beloved players. As a rookie with Pittsburgh, Harris played in fourteen games and rushed for 1,055 yards with thirteen touchdowns and was named Rookie of the Year by *The Sporting News* and UPI. He was particularly popular with the Italian-American fans in Pittsburgh, who became known as "Franco's Italian Army" because they wore army helmets with his number on them.

Throughout his thirteen-year NFL career, he rushed for 12,120 yards and scored ninety-one rushing touchdowns. In eight of his thirteen seasons, he rushed for more than 1,000 yards, breaking Jim Brown's record. He was chosen for nine consecutive Pro Bowls and was All-Pro in 1977. He helped the Steelers win four Super Bowls between

1974 and 1979. During those four Super Bowls, Harris rushed for 354 yards on 101 carries (Super Bowl records) and had four touchdowns, which ties for the second most in Super Bowl history.

Harris was the key to one of the most famous plays in professional football called the "Immaculate Reception." In a 1972 playoff game with the Oakland Raiders, the Steelers were trailing the Raiders seven to six. When a Terry Bradshaw pass was deflected by defensive back Jack Tatum, Harris grabbed the ball just before it hit the ground and ran it in for a game-winning touchdown with twenty-two seconds left in the game. Harris was the MVP of the Super Bowl in 1975 and was inducted into the Pro Football Hall of Fame in 1990.

"I was born in Fort Dix, New Jersey, and grew up in Mt. Holly, New Jersey. I've got four brothers and four sisters, and I'm the third oldest. My mother was a housewife, and my father was in the military for a number of years, then took a job as a supervisor at a local hospital near Fort Dix.

"As children, we were very active, and we grew up in an active neighborhood. There were a number of kids in the neighborhood. Just about every day we would play baseball in one of the vacant lots in the neighborhood. We just picked teams, and I remember that being a lot of fun. At night, we would go out and play games like hide-and-seek, and we were always racing.

"I remember there were two cracks in the road, and we would race from crack-to-crack. When I was around eight or nine, my older sister would always beat me, and my goal was to beat her! Finally, when I was ten, I was able to beat her racing. There was always a lot of activity in our neighborhood. We played kickball, rode bikes, and other things. But we never did really play football. We had a television, but I can't remember ever watching sports because we were always outside playing while the sports shows were on.

"I was about eight years old when I played my first organized sport, baseball. And that was the only organized sport I played in my first six years of school. I enjoyed baseball, and I was pretty good at it, but I don't recall anyone or anything in particular that influenced me to play. I guess it was just the kind of thing everybody was doing. I've never really thought about why I started playing. It just seems like that was something I always did. Of course, being a good athlete helped a lot, because I was able to pick up things rather quickly in sports.

"The Little League team used to take us to see a Philadelphia baseball game every year. That was the highlight of the summer. We always had seats in the left field, and one of our big things was to see how close to the dugout we could get so we could see the players. We used to find ways to do that, and it was a big thrill, trying to get close to see the big players. That trip was always a big inspiration. I remember thinking about wanting to be a baseball player when I grew up. I can remember pretending I was so-and-so baseball player when I played. But that was just more of a dream, not really believing that was going to happen.

"My parents didn't have much of a role in my athletics. They weren't able to attend many sporting events. My dad worked, and my mother was from Italy. The only sport she really saw in Italy was soccer, and even that wasn't that big when she lived there. Occasionally, my dad would come to a baseball game.

"In high school, my parents would come see me play football once in a while. My mother didn't understand the game and to this day still doesn't, so it was difficult for her to understand what was going on in the game and to follow it. But both of my parents always felt very proud of us for competing, and just about everyone in the family was a good athlete.

"I don't remember any particular words of advice or encouragement from my parents about sports. With nine kids in the family, the focus seemed to point more toward whoever the baby was at the time. For my mother, that was her primary focus, and there was always a baby around during those times. Plus, my mother had to learn English when she came to America, and those early years were hard for her, so she wasn't able to be involved and be active in our sports pursuits. Basically, sports were just something that I did, and my parents didn't have any direction or influence on that. I just went where the other guys were and starting playing. We just went down to the park and played.

"As far as my values are concerned, especially the values you learn early on, I enjoyed a great, stable family. My mom was always around. I know that's not always the case today, but my mom was always there, and my dad was home every night. There were certain expectations, and my dad was pretty strict on things like when you were to be home and what kind of grades you got in school.

"Plus, we had a lot of good people in the neighborhood. I really enjoyed the people in our neighborhood. I enjoyed my childhood and associated with a lot of good people. My parents were good parents who cared for their family and that set the foundation. And, I'll have to admit, we also had a great public school system that had a big influence on me.

"I had some great coaches and teachers who had a lot to do with my development as an athlete and an individual. I started playing football in the seventh grade, and the coaches were just fantastic, and I thoroughly enjoyed playing. I also had a teacher in junior high school who got us involved in the community doing charitable things and finding ways to raise money to help other people. I guess that laid the groundwork for my interest to always be involved in the community. That all started because of a teacher I had in the seventh grade.

"In high school I played football my freshman year, and that was rough. We had a tough coach. There were many practices I didn't think I was going to make it. He drilled us and worked us hard. But we had a great class of guys on the team, and we went undefeated that year. I also played basketball my freshman year in high school and did well enough to make the varsity team. I think I was the first freshman to ever make the varsity team. I liked football, but I didn't love it at that point, so I thought basketball might be the way for me to go, to play and excel in.

"Then, during my sophomore year, when my brother was a senior, I learned that he got a football scholarship. I was totally surprised and amazed that there was such a thing as a football scholarship—I'd never heard of that. People around me told me that if you do well in football, you could go to college, and I was just flabbergasted that somebody in our family was going to college. That's something we never dreamed about and never planned to do. And here it was, because of football.

"My brother had a chance to go to college, and I was really taken by that, just amazed that something like this could actually be real. I was just like, Wow! My brother is going to college and people are telling me that I could actually get a scholarship, too, if I was a good player. So, that kind of set a goal for me.

"My junior year, I made the High School All-American team. That was probably the first time I ever set a goal for myself and set out to pursue the goal because I saw it as an attainable goal, a real possibility. It was something I'd never even dreamed about before. When I saw that something like this could actually happen, it just changed my entire perspective.

"I played three sports in high school, basketball, baseball, and football. In high school, basketball was my first love and football was my third. But, if I would have just played the sport that I loved the most, I would have never found out how good I would have been at football. By playing all three, I found the sport I excelled at, even though I liked the other sports better. Eventually, I came to love football more than the other sports, but initially it was the other way around. If I hadn't played them all, I would never have known which sport I was really good at.

"I don't recall any specific words of wisdom from my coaches. I'm sure some were said, but nothing really stuck with me. I look at the total actions over the years, and our coaches were wonderful. I had great coaches who were good people, who tried to set good examples and cared for their players. And that's how the school and teachers were, too. It was great. I enjoyed the teachers. The level of education was great, and my classmates were just incredible. It was a wonderful experience. We had one of those unbelievable classes filled with wonderful people who ended up doing many wonderful things in so many different directions. I'm lucky to have been in the right place at the right time with the right people.

"Part of my character that enabled me to achieve what I've achieved relates to the setting of goals. When I set a goal and decided that I wanted to accomplish something, it really made a difference. When I didn't set goals I might do okay, but I wouldn't achieve that higher potential, that step above that takes you to a new level. Goals create challenges—more than challenges that deal with the circumstances around me—more of a challenge within and the determination to rise to that challenge. More than anything, I would say it's that internal challenge that allowed me to push beyond my limitations and achieve more.

"Even when something negative happens, I challenge myself. Sometimes, when something bad happens, people succumb to the circumstance and totally give in and give up. With me, it's the complete opposite. If something negative happens, I fight through it and hopefully succeed beyond expectations. I think that makes you a stronger individual. To work through the challenge creates a deeper dimension to your life.

"As far as value systems are concerned, I definitely think that by the time you're around ten or twelve years old you know some things about right and wrong, and that you do make certain decisions. I also think that who you surround yourself with plays a big role on how your value and ethical systems develop. Sometimes the people you surround yourself with get to be a big part of the problem. At a certain point in your life you simply have to realize certain things. Most of us pick up some good values as a kid, but you have to use your head and realize there are some things to leave behind if you want to go forward and go certain places and do certain things.

"All of us are exposed to certain environments that might not be healthy in a lot of ways. Sometimes those environments can consume someone and totally destroy them, and sometimes those challenges can make someone even stronger. Unfortunately, people are exposed to experiences and environments that they have no control over. One would hope that the positive influence of sports could give them a better opportunity, or basis, to be able to overcome some of the more negative aspects that might happen in other parts of their lives.

"There are a lot of mentors out there, who through their actions or words, can make a difference in someone's life. It might be just one little thing they say or do that can set a new direction for someone or create a new goal for someone.

"You never know what might happen, but to me, there's no doubt that athletics creates opportunities for people that might not otherwise be available. For example, had it not been for the scholarship my brother got, the entire direction of my family might have been different. It not only changed the direction of my life, but it changed the direction for my entire family and generations of my family to come. All of my brothers and sisters do well, and the kids automatically go to college now. That's not even a question anymore. None of that was real, and we would have never even thought about it if my brother hadn't gotten that scholarship.

"As far as any advice I have for parents, I think it would be great to give your kids the chance to play more than one sport. Sometimes kids think they're good at something because they like it. Maybe they don't know their true talents yet and don't realize what's possible.

"Try not to exert too much pressure on your kid to perform or play a sport they don't want to. For me, it worked really well that my parents weren't parents who went crazy over my playing sports. I got to make my own decisions. My folks let me do my own thing and have fun doing it, and that was great for me. Some other kids might need more direction than I got, but parents have to know their children and meet their needs, not the parents' needs."

* * *

A lot of people might think that Franco Harris is one lucky individual. He was born with incredible physical skills. He was a star athlete in high school and college. He was one of the best running backs to ever play professional football. He's even got a statue of himself in the Pittsburgh Airport depicting his famous "Immaculate Reception." But the success of Franco Harris doesn't have anything to do with luck.

Like many kids, Franco had childhood dreams of being a star athlete. But, unlike many kids, Franco took his dream to the next level and made a decision—a choice—that he was going to do the things that were required to realize his dream. Franco Harris had a change of mind about the world of possibilities around him.

It's been said that nothing is more powerful than a change of mind— "no economic, political, or military power can compare with the power of a change of mind" (*Global Mind Change;* Willis Harmen). Once you commit, really commit to a decision, you divorce yourself from any other possibility. It's not a wish or a preference anymore. It's the unwavering will and desire to rise to the challenge and attain the goal you've set, through persistent and intelligent action.

Anyone can tap into the power of commitment, because it works in every aspect of life, not just sports. In virtually all cases, the person who succeeds is the person who understands and exercises commitment. You don't climb mountains with one giant leap. You do it step by step. It's the person who keeps stepping, in spite of the hardships, who gets to see the view from the top. You can call that lucky, but luck comes to those who make it.

Chapter 10

Deacon Jones

It's not the mountain we conquer, but ourselves.
— **Sir Edmund Hillary**

avid D. "Deacon" Jones was born in Eatonville, Florida, on December 9, 1938. He was drafted in 1961, in the fourteenth round by the L.A. Rams. He played for the Rams (1961 to 1971), the San Diego Chargers (1972-1973) and the Washington Redskins (1974). He was a flamboyant player and dubbed himself "Deacon" because he believed no one would ever remember him with a name like David.

Deacon is considered by many to be the best defensive end ever to play professional football. The term "quarterback sack" is attributed to Deacon, something he did extremely well and often during his fourteen-year career. Unofficially, he accumulated twenty-six sacks in 1967, which would be the single season record for sacks.

He played college football at South Carolina State and Mississippi Vocational at the tackle position. While scouting a defensive player from Mississippi Vocational, Ram scouts noticed this huge (6´5´´, 272 pounds) guy catch a tackle-eligible pass and out run the defensive back. That was Deacon Jones, and the scouts drafted Deacon instead of the defensive back.

For ten seasons, Jones and teammate Merlin Olsen combined to give the Rams a devastatingly effective left side dubbed as the famous "Fearsome Foursome," one of the premier defensive lines of all time.

Jones was an eight-time Pro Bowl and All-Pro selection. He received the George S. Halas trophy in 1967 and 1968. He was named to the

NFL's 75th Anniversary All-Time team in 1994. In 1999, he was ranked number 13 on *The Sporting News'* list of the 100 Greatest Football Players. In 1980, his first year of eligibility, he was elected to the Pro Football Hall of Fame.

In addition to numerous other awards and recognitions, Jones has worked as a television actor and appeared in numerous TV programs since the 1970s. Currently, he serves as the president and CEO of the Deacon Jones Foundation, an organization he founded in 1977 to assist young people with a comprehensive program that includes education, mentoring, corporate internship, and community service.

" **I** was born in Eatonville, Florida, in 1938. That's a little town outside of Orlando. The year I was born, society was quite a bit different than it is today in America. We lived in a segregated environment, and I think that drew our family closer. I had five sisters and two brothers, along with both of my parents. During that era, we certainly needed togetherness, and our family had a lot of love and respect for each other.

"My father was a common laborer, and my mother was a maid. They both had a limited educational background, but they passed on to us what they knew best, namely, discipline. My parents used a real staunch discipline approach, and I would say that's the single most important thing that enabled me to have the opportunities that I've had.

"The neighborhood I grew up in was unique, and it still remains the only all-black community that's chartered and incorporated in the United States. We grew up playing and doing everything as a family first, because we didn't have any other amenities like nice parks to play in. You had to make your own fun, so to speak. We played in the neighbor's yard, the street, or the vacant lot.

"We organized all of our games internally. We didn't have a park and recreation department to help us. In spite of the circumstances, that was probably the most fun I've ever had. I thought it was the greatest thing in the world, to be able to compete against your family or neighbors, going at it tooth and nail. It was like every game was a Super Bowl, and every play was important. That just goes to show you that you can get along in life with a lot less than you think you can.

"I was the third youngest of the children. I had one sister and one brother who were younger than me. My father was a sports-minded kind of person, so both my brothers and I played football. That was like a requirement in our family, whether you liked it or not, you had to play football. My father insisted upon it. We were going to play football, no questions asked. That's just the way it was in my house.

"My father believed that football would help instill some rigid discipline in us and that we would learn the basic fundamentals of how to get along and live with other people. He also believed that football would bring out the toughness in us. He believed it helped us understand two basic fundamentals of life, commitment and responsibility. I think it would be great if we could emphasize those two traits more today, because those are two areas that we all face every day.

"I didn't really want to play football at first. I didn't see any sense in getting the heck knocked out of you. I would rather have played baseball or basketball. As a kid, I never would have chosen football as my primary sport. But things changed after I got my first lick in on the football field, and I found out that I liked the game. I had a reputation as a hard-hitter in the NFL, and most people wouldn't believe that I really didn't want to play football as a kid because I didn't see much sense in getting hit.

"I grew up in a very competitive environment. My younger brother was probably the most competitive of all of us. He hated it when I would do anything better than him, and that lasted all the way to when we played together one year with the Los Angeles Rams. He was an animal! I was a little more respectful of my older brother. I was more an admirer of him, and he was really the only idol I had to look up to in the environment we lived in.

"My younger brother, Harold, was probably the best athlete in the family. He went to Grambling College and played football, and he was an awesome high school basketball player. My older brother graduated from Xavier University in New Orleans, where he played football, but he didn't go on to the pros.

"My father was a pretty good baseball player. But he had limited knowledge of how to prepare for the next level, and from a technical point of view, he only had limited information he could give to me to help me prepare for the next level. From a personal point of view, he offered me a lot of encouragement. He would watch all of my practices and go to all of our games, at every level. He was always there to be a support vehicle.

"We had to find out all the technical things about our game from the coaches we had and from reading about sports and watching them on television. But I believe that my father's love and attention is at the core of my success. His being there inspired me. Just to see him standing on the sideline when I was in high school or college gave me all the inspiration I needed. It was great to have the kind of encouragement, like when he would put his arms around my neck and tell me that I could accomplish whatever I wanted to do.

"Jackie Robinson was my athletic role model. Eventually, I got to meet him and became friends with him over the years before he passed away. When I was twelve years old, I saw him play in Orlando, and that really inspired me. My buddies and I used to go down to the stadium and sneak through the fence and go to the games. We got a chance to go back to the locker room and meet Jackie one time. He had a long conversation with us, and that had a big impact on me. That was a real satisfying encounter for me.

"And it was kind of a unique situation. Mr. Robinson was sliding into second base and got spiked by the second baseman. His hands were bleeding, and he went back to the locker room, and my buddies and me followed him down there. When he came out, he stood there and talked to us. He gave us some advice, too. He told us to do our best and be the best we could be.

"Segregation created some nasty situations back then. We had to sit in the black section of the ballpark, and we weren't allowed in certain areas. So Jackie Robinson paid special attention to us black kids. He would talk to us and give us autographs.

"I was kind of a brash kid back then, with a loud mouth. I remember telling Jackie that I was going to be better than him. I remember him just looking back at me with that big smile of his, and he patted me on the head. Years later, I was playing in a golf tournament that Jackie was playing in, too. I walked up to him and met him on the tee. You know, he remembered that conversation we had when I was twelve years old, and that was a really exciting moment for me.

"From a personal point of view, I would say that my dad was my primary role model. He was the guy I looked up to and was the guy I was trained to respect. We didn't have many choices for role models in the environment I grew up in. There were very few black idols back then, and the other athletic role models I had were mostly guys in the Negro Baseball League whom few people would know today. But my father led the pack as far as role models are concerned. I believed in him. I followed whatever he said. My thought patterns were elevated to new levels because he wanted me to have the opportunities that he never got.

"As I progressed through my life, going to segregated schools and things of that nature, I had some ideas in my mind about what kind of future I wanted. I was fortunate to have been born with some athletic skill, and I understood that the only way I was probably going to have a chance at success was through the education I could get playing athletics.

"I attended segregated schools at the high school and college level. I was drafted by the L.A. Rams right out of college at Mississippi Vocational College. That was a tough time for me because I had it set in my mind that I had one chance, one thing, one opportunity, and one option. And that's a dangerous thing, to only allow yourself one option. If I hadn't been drafted by the Rams, I don't know what I would have done.

"In my work with inner city kids, I try to stress to those kids to expose themselves to as many things as they can in their youth. Don't lock yourself into something real early in life because you might find something better to commit your mind and heart to later. More exposure to different things creates more choices and better chances at being successful. I only had one card to play, and I was lucky enough for that to work out. But I don't advocate that approach. If you only have one card to play, you have a greater chance to lose than you have to win.

"In a sense, life is just a series of different moments. Everyone has individual, personal moments. Some of us seize the moment and take it to the next level, and some of us don't recognize the moment at all. A lot of us miss our opportunities because we're blind as a bat. As I look back at my life and the one option I perceived that I had, I had to seize each moment that moved me in the direction I wanted to go. One stage was getting drafted. Another stage was getting assigned to the team, preparing myself and optimizing the one opportunity I had. I was lucky that the Rams needed everything when I was drafted, and that created more opportunity for me, and I seized the moment. I made the team as an offensive tackle. Most people don't know that I started my first NFL game as an offensive tackle against the Pittsburgh Steelers.

"In talking about significant moments in my life, Coach George Allen comes to mind. I was at a point where I needed to expand my potential as a player and he came into my life and helped me expand my game to the maximum level, both physically and mentally. I don't know if I would have ever reached my full potential without his entering my life. I respected him just like I respected my father, and I give him all the credit for helping me take my game to the next level.

"I've got to give some credit to my high school coach for my success, too. But it's not credit for something positive that I got from him. My high school coach was a former All-American at Florida A&M University. Coach didn't think I was good enough to be recommended for a scholarship to A&M. The only college offer I ended up getting was from South Carolina State.

"I didn't find out about his not recommending me until I was already playing pro ball. I mean, he was an All-American from A&M

and had relationships with the coaches there. He gave me no credit at all. He wouldn't accept me, and he wouldn't recommend me. That was a little disappointing.

"Before my high school coach died, he told me that the reason he didn't recommend me for a scholarship was that he didn't believe my commitment to football was strong enough. After I made the team as a L.A. Ram, I went back home and asked him, Do I satisfy your thought process now? He didn't have anything to say to that. As I look back, he doubted me all the way. That probably had to do with something he didn't like about my personality. So, while my high school coach didn't contribute positive elements to my career, he sure motivated me to prove him wrong.

"As far as football being fun for me, I took a little different outlook than that. I grew up with a lot of dislike for society and the inequality of the situation. Football became an outlet for me. I got the opportunity to get all that anger out of my heart and soul by having the chance to participate in a physical sport.

"Football was always a personal item for me. As a pro, I separated the monetary value from the game and held the game in the highest esteem. I put forth my best effort every time out. Playing with an injury was like a badge of courage. All the guys I played with, especially the Fearsome Foursome, had that same attitude. To compete under impossible circumstances was the number one thing in a game. We were always there for each other.

"I learned to play the game differently than it's played now. I had a love for it, respect for it, and I separated the money part from it. The way we played had nothing to do with money. My attitude was, If I'm putting on my uniform and going out on the field, you better lock and load, baby. It didn't have anything to do with money. It had to do with me being the best football player I could be.

"It was important to me to be able to dominate my game and do everything above and beyond the call of duty. My commitment came from the heart and soul of my father teaching me to be the best I can be. I wasn't going out there unless I could be the best I could be. I walked away from professional football without an injury or a mark when I could no longer be the best defensive end in the league.

"My inspiration came from living under the conditions that I had to live under and the opportunities that were denied to me because of the color of my skin. When the opportunity to compete at the highest level came around, there wasn't a man alive who was more ready than I was. All the anger I had, I turned toward the game and used it to reach the heights of my game. I learned so much. This game gave me so much training and direction. It was better than any college education, because it was on-the-job training.

"I started to associate all the different pieces of life. I did all the things that I was supposed to do, and I did them because the thing that was driving me internally was to help change society. Football was my only way to make a positive contribution. I used every ounce of the time I spent in professional football making a better person out of myself, and I reached down and tried to pull as many people up the ladder of success as I possibly could in the time I've lived on this planet. I'm thrilled about my contribution, and I've worked out all of my problems. I got all the anger out through professional football and through beating the brains out of every man who ever lined up in front of me!

"As far as my core values are concerned, I absolutely believe that these were set by my parents, beginning on the day the doctor slapped me on the butt. That's when our values need to start being put together. We lived a life of discipline. We went to church because that was part of our household living condition. As kids, we had no choice in the matter.

"I would say before a child is fourteen, their core values are in place. That kid is already somebody and has his core values, good or bad, that he's gotten from someone—parents, teachers, neighbors, whomever. If he isn't under control by then, there's a good chance that the parents and the law are going to have to work together.

"I run the Deacon Jones Foundation, which is a community program that deals with smart, inner city kids. We take these kids and develop their needs under a specialized program. You have to include discipline in their lives. You have to teach kids to respect other people. They must understand responsibility, and they must understand commitment.

"One out of every two kids I work with in the inner city comes from a single-parent household. That's a problem, because kids need a male influence in their lives, too. And kids are spending a lot more time alone and unsupervised. For example, so many kids spend a lot of time on the computer where it's difficult to monitor what they're getting involved with, and that's hurting a lot of kids. We need to get better control of that.

"The more things you make a child complete, the better off the child is. Sometimes you have to force the action and you have to be willing and able to do that, if it's needed. You've got to get the foundational traits into these kids while they're still young. Once they have those traits, all the little things that happen to young people and all the little misgivings that come up in life can be dealt with when they already have a strong foundation."

* * *

L ife is…the opportunities you recognize, seize, and bring to fruition through your attentions, efforts, and actions. It (life) can't be any more or any less than that. Just like the line from an old Pink Floyd song that talks about how all you touch and see, is all your life will be. And, perhaps, the most important part of that line is *what you see*, for what you *see* becomes that to which your attention is directed.

If we pay particular attention to a thing or thought, we tend to create a habit-pattern about that particular thing or thought. You probably put your first shoe on the same foot each morning, and you probably take the same route to work each day. And you do these things without any thought. At one point you did think about them, but having repeatedly done them becomes the proverbial "riding a bike" story. You repetitively have a thought and perform an action until it's preformed at an unconscious level. You've become the thought.

There's always the opportunity to have contrasting thoughts about any given circumstance. For example, if you're involved in some demanding circumstance, your mind will conjure up one of two variations of these thoughts: *This is really hard, and I would be much more comfortable quitting* or *This is really hard, but I'm going to give my best effort because I know there's a reward of some kind.*

It's pretty evident that Deacon Jones took the latter course. Sure, he was aware that he didn't have the same opportunities as most other kids. While he grew up in the land of the free and the land of plenty, I'm sure most all of our childhoods were filled with more freedom and plenty than he ever got to experience. But Deacon Jones opened the door when opportunity came knocking, in spite of all of his disadvantages.

He paid attention and gave his unswerving attention to the one choice he perceived he had in this life. He became his thought, and that manifested itself as one of the best professional football players in history, and as an individual who takes deep pride in helping those less fortunate learn how to direct their attentions to loftier objectives.

Chapter 11

LEROY KELLY

What you get by achieving your goals is not as important as what you become by achieving your goals.
— *Johann Wolfgang von Goethe*

L eroy Kelly was born on May 20, 1942, in Philadelphia, Pennsylvania. He attended Simon Gratz High School and Morgan State University in Baltimore, Maryland. He was drafted by the Cleveland Browns in 1964 in the eighth round. He was the 110th pick. He played with the Browns until 1973. He also played one year (1974) with the Chicago Fire of the now defunct World Football League.

Kelly was noted as an exceptionally fine runner on the muddy playing fields of his time. At six feet and 202 pounds, he was very effective on the famous Browns trap plays and equally devastating on sweeps and as a receiver. His quickness, balance, and evasive style kept him relatively injury free, and he only missed four games during his ten-year career as a professional football player.

When Leroy Kelly entered the NFL, he was a backup running back to the great Jim Brown for his first two years. When Brown retired, Kelly filled the void in a manner not often seen in professional football. His combined career yardage is second only to Jim Brown's for the Cleveland Browns.

Kelly rushed for 7,274 yards during his career. He averaged 4.2 yards per carry and amassed seventy-four touchdowns. Including punt returns and receptions, his total combined yards are 12,329.

Kelly won NFL rushing titles in 1967 and 1968. He was a two-time punt return champion in 1965 and 1971. He was named All-NFL five times and named to six Pro Bowls. He was named to the NFL's All-Decade Team and won the Bert Bell Award in 1968. He was inducted into the Pro Football Hall of Fame in 1994.

"I was born in Philadelphia. I was the next to the youngest child out of nine kids in our family. My mom was a home-maker, and my dad worked at several different jobs. My folks came to Philadelphia from the South. My father came up first and got a job, then my mom came up, and that's when they got married.

"My dad did all kinds of different things, but his primary job was in a lime quarry where he worked as a machinist. My mom had her hands full taking care of all us kids.

"Growing up, I was closest to my younger brother, Pat, and my sister, May. May and I were born on the same day, two years apart. The rest of the kids were older and either getting married or going off into the service, so they weren't really around that much when I and the younger kids were growing up. I lost my oldest brother and one of my sisters before I was actually born. So, there were seven kids in the house, but my closest relationships were with Pat and May.

"My brother Pat and I were very competitive and competed in just about every venue. I remember we had one of those electric foot-ball games with the plastic players. Pat and I would stay down in the cellar for hours playing that little electric football game. We played many different kinds of games in the neighborhood. Whatever was the game of the day, we were playing it.

"We lived in a pretty unique neighborhood. There were only three rows of houses in our neighborhood, with about fifty houses in each row. We had a large park right down the street. For us, it was almost like a country club atmosphere. It was a mixed-race neighborhood with a large cross section of different people.

"We were always playing some kind of pickup game. We would play football, but we didn't have a real football. We would take a Sunday paper and tie it up so we could throw it. That was our football. The older kids had a real football, and we got to play touch football with them on Sundays. But, for us younger kids, we just had to make do with whatever we had. We stayed pretty active, and the playground was where everybody converged.

"I grew up in the same neighborhood until I went to college. While I was in college, my brother signed with the Kansas City Royals, and they gave him enough money to buy my parents a nicer, new house. That was about my junior year in college.

"When I was about ten or eleven years old I started playing organized baseball. I didn't play organized football until I went to high school. As far as any influences to play sports, that's just what everybody did. The older kids did it, and we just followed in their footsteps. It was just our natural progression.

"My parents didn't really have much of an influence on my athletic career. My dad was known as a pretty good athlete, but he worked so much that he didn't have much time to spend with us kids playing games. We learned more from the older kids in the neighborhood. That's basically how we picked up most of our skills.

"But my parents always respected our choices to play sports. It was always our choice as to whether or not we wanted to play something. Occasionally, my mom might have a few concerns about me playing football. You know how moms can be about things like that. But it was always my choice to play or not play.

"Something one of my older brothers did had a big influence on me in regard to sports. Our high school, Simon Gratz, hadn't won a football game in about twelve years. My brother scored a touchdown for their first win in all those years, and there was an article and picture of my brother in the local paper. My mom cut that article out of the paper, and she would let me read it and look at the picture of my brother. That really inspired me. He served as a good athletic role model for me.

"My primary ethical role models were definitely my parents. There was a big spiritual influence in our family. My parents were involved in the church and naturally brought us into that environment. We went to church and Sunday School and did other church-based activities. We learned a lot by knowing the Lord and religion. It helped us set our values and morals at a young age.

"My dad had an incredible work ethic. There would be a foot of snow, or more, on the ground, and my dad would be putting chains on the tires just trying to get to work. When he would get there, he would be one of the only people who showed up, even though there wouldn't really be any work being done because everybody else couldn't get there. But he would punch the time clock anyway. I guess they paid him for his time just for showing up.

"I got a lot of support from my high school football coach, too. Coach Lorenz played a big part in my success as an athlete. I played quarterback in high school and was the captain of the team. Coach Lorenz helped me be a leader for our team and gave the whole squad an overall sense of team, and he provided us with the tools to have a pretty good team. There's no doubt that Coach Lorenz had a positive impact on my life.

"Coach also was instrumental in my future success as a football player. He was the primary reason I got to go to college. He contacted a lot of schools on my behalf, and he's the one who really got me a college scholarship to play football. Had I not got the scholarship, I would have never played professional football, and who knows what direction my life would have taken.

"It's interesting to look back on all of this. Back in high school, and even in college, I never really aspired to play professional football. I didn't even watch football that much. Actually, I had more expectations of playing professional baseball, because I was a very good baseball player. But that didn't work out because the college I went to didn't have a baseball program. You might say I just went along with the show, and the show happened to be football.

"Basically, I was in college playing football and just trying to get through. I didn't have any real expectations that I might be able to play professional football until my junior year in college. I started receiving a few questionnaires from some pro teams, but it was really my head coach at college who got me drafted by Cleveland.

"My college coach was a good friend of Buddy Young, a scout for the Baltimore Colts. During my senior year, the Colts were looking at someone else, but Buddy Young told the Browns about me. That's how the Browns found out about me because they hadn't scouted me. The Browns sent a scout to the Orange Blossom Classic we were playing in, and I guess my performance that day was good enough for them to draft me into their organization.

"Looking back, a lot of my success had to do with the neighborhood I grew up in, and the big park that was just down the street from my house. As kids, we stayed in that park just about all day. Like I said before, it was our country club. We had just about everything we needed in that park. We learned social skills, athletic skills, leadership skills, and a lot of other things that helped us prepare for life. And the atmosphere of the park and the neighborhood was as good as it gets.

"Back in our neighborhood, we didn't have to worry about drugs or stealing. Nobody ever locked the door at night. Sometimes, people wouldn't even close their doors. That's how we grew up. And there was a lot of respect around our neighborhood. If you met someone walking down the street, you would address that person as Mr. or Mrs. Whomever. And if you were doing something you weren't supposed to be doing, any adult in the neighborhood wouldn't think twice about correcting you. It's a different world now. Kids today live in a different world.

"A lot of the things we learned as kids, we learned from the older kids in the neighborhood. Our parents were usually working, so we didn't see them much during the day, and we rarely played any kind of games or sports with the adults. The older kids were role models for us. Some of them were even like fathers to us, in the sense that they taught us about sports and competition, having good morals, and doing the right thing. It was easy for us growing up. We had a perfect environment.

"Today, society doesn't seem to have as high a regard for respect and discipline as we had when we were kids. If we got out of line as kids, we got a whipping, and we understood completely that we were doing something we weren't supposed to be doing. We understood that we were going to show respect to other people and do the right things or pay a price. Now, if you spank your kids, you might end up in jail, and kids today are smart enough to know that if they get a spanking, they can tell somebody and get that parent in trouble.

"You hear it over and over again, but you've got to talk to your kids. You have to talk with them and not at them. A lot of parents don't want to talk about certain things with their kids, but you've got to talk to them about life and the things that go on in life. Your kids are going to make decisions anyway. What you do and what you say as parents has a huge impact on how your kids are going to think about something and what kind of choice they're going to make. Everything is a choice, and as a parent, you just hope that you've given your kids the right inputs to help them make the right choices. It's as simple as that."

* * *

There's an old Chinese saying that states, "A bird does not sing because it has an answer. It sings because it has a song." If you're fortunate enough to have awoken to the symphony of songbirds on a cool spring morning, you'll certainly appreciate the quality, clarity, and tone that provides an avian concerto for you to enjoy.

If music is the purest form of expression, then surely the notes of a songbird approach perfection, not for the purpose of finding solutions or answers; only for the purpose of singing their song. That's just what songbirds do. That's their character.

In a sense, songbirds have some attractive advantages over human beings. They don't have any concept of fashion. They don't worry about a mortgage or the price of gas. Being popular or cool isn't even an afterthought, and they're not worried at all about scheduling their vacation next month. They don't have these concerns because all they're concerned with is what's going on at the present moment.

There's a sense of quality in everything a songbird does. Free from the trappings of human beings, songbirds are connected to the present moment. They show up for work attitudinally dressed to play. They don't make plans to be successful. They are successful.

On occasion, human beings get a glimpse of living in the present moment, where time and ego take a back seat to simply being...being what you can at a particular moment when all the external and internal noises of life stop for a moment and release the onerous chains that bind our potential to excel and expand.

No doubt, Leroy Kelly had his share of those particular moments, where time stood still and his entire focus was totally wrapped up in a football play that lasts eight seconds. He wasn't looking for any answers on those days. He was just singing the song he knew how to sing. And he sang it well. That's just what he did. That was his character.

Chapter 12

Paul Krause

The average estimate themselves by what they do,
the above average by what they are.
— *Johann Friedrich Von Schiller*

aul James Krause was born in Flint, Michigan, on February 19, 1942. Krause was an outstanding high school athlete at Bendle High School in Burton, Michigan, and earned All-State honors in basketball, football, baseball, and track.

Paul played college football at the University of Iowa and was a two-way starter as a wide receiver and defensive back. He was selected for the East-West Shrine Game, the Coaches' All-American Game, and the College All-Star Game.

He also played baseball at Iowa, and as a sophomore, earned All-American honors and was drafted into the major leagues. Krause turned down the offer to play professional baseball, and his baseball opportunities ended when he suffered a shoulder injury in his junior year at Iowa playing football.

Krause was drafted in the second round of the NFL Draft in 1964 by the Washington Redskins and played defensive back. In his rookie season, he led the NFL with twelve interceptions, including interceptions in seven straight games. As a rookie, he was named to the All-NFL first team and also participated in his first of eight Pro Bowl appearances. In 1968, he was traded to the Minnesota Vikings.

Krause played for the Vikings until he retired after the 1979 season and was one of the few players to make appearances in all four of the Vikings Super Bowl appearances. He was often referred to as the

Vikings "Center Fielder" because of his success at collegiate baseball and his ability to make interceptions.

Krause holds the all-time record for interceptions in the NFL, where he hawked a total of eighty-one interceptions. In his sixteen-year career, he only missed two games due to injury. He was named to the Iowa Sports Hall of Fame in 1985, named All-NFL four times, All-NFC five times, All-Eastern Conference twice, and was inducted into the Pro Football Hall of Fame in 1998.

" I was born in Flint, Michigan. I've got two older brothers, an older sister, and a younger sister. I was fourth in line. My father worked for the 7-Up bottling company, and my mother stayed home and took care of the kids and the house.

"My brothers and older sister all competed in sports. Both of my brothers played baseball, football, and basketball. One of my brothers was an All-Conference quarterback in high school. They were several years older than me, but they would let me compete with them sometimes, so there was a degree of competitiveness around our house.

"The neighborhood I grew up in was a conservative, poor, white neighborhood. As kids, we spent a lot of time outside playing pickup games. That's really all we had to do, and there was always some kind of game going on. We didn't have many of the recreational facilities that kids have today, but we managed to play some kind of sport all the time.

"The first organized sport I played was baseball. I was seven years old then. After that, we went to football, then to basketball. It wasn't organized sports like we have today with kids. Our organization was basically a teacher trying to put together some teams, and we just went out and played a particular sport.

"As far as any influence I had to play sports, I don't know that there's any specific example I could refer to. My dad played baseball in high school, and my brothers were athletes. I'm sure that had some influence on me. But I think the biggest thing was that was what everybody else was doing, and we didn't have many other things to do back then. It just seemed like the thing to do.

"I used to hang around the athletic fields and the football fields and watch the older kids play. My athletic heroes were the great baseball players like Willie Mays, Mickey Mantle, Ted Williams, and DiMaggio. Those were the guys you wanted to be like when you were a kid.

"Whether or not I played was always my decision. My mom and dad never told me I couldn't play, and they never really pushed me to play. They enjoyed my playing, but they didn't attend too many games. I remember my dad did come to a basketball game in high school when I scored sixty-four points.

"My grandfather attended more games than my parents did. I remember him being at just about every baseball game I played in high school. But my dad was working, and my mom was taking care of the house. It was just different back then in the fifties.

"My parents were my primary moral role models. They set the rules and the tone of how it was at our house. We were a very religious family. Church wasn't just something our family did every now and then. It was part of our family routine, and we were in church on a regular basis.

"I remember when I was in about the ninth grade my mom wouldn't let me go to basketball practice on Wednesdays because that was a church night for us. As things progressed and my athletic activities advanced, I finally got to make all the practices, even on Wednesday.

"We came from a strict family, and I believe that had a major influence on my moral fiber. I can also remember that if I did something wrong, I got the business end of a razor strap. Believe me, it hurt at the time, but it sure taught me respect. I don't think there's anything wrong with that.

"My religious background carried over into my athletics, and the respect thing was very important. You had to respect everybody, whether it was a teammate, coach, opponent, or anyone else. If you didn't show the proper respect, you'd hear about it.

"I don't recall any significant input that my high school coach had on my character development. We came from a small school with about 300 total students. My football coach was also my baseball and basketball coach. So, being from a small school, if you had any talent at all, you typically played a sport. The coach gave us the opportunity to participate, and because it was a small school a lot of kids got some exposure to sports that might not have at a bigger school.

"I think the success I had with athletics is a combination of a lot of things. My family background, my siblings, my interest in sports, and a lot of other things contributed to my success. I think a great athlete is born with a certain degree of athletic ability, and if a person like that works hard and focuses, he'll perform better than someone else with the same level of ability who hasn't put in the work. There's a certain level of ability that some have and some don't, and some of that just can't be taught. Average ability athletes can be taught to be good athletes, but you can't teach God-given ability.

"I was pretty lucky as far as sports are concerned. I could play just about any sport that I picked up. I think I had some God-given ability, and I've always been thankful for that. In the pros, I also think that I saw the game a little differently than a lot of people did. I think I understood the game better than a lot of my opponents. I think that's why I got all the interceptions that I did. I had a knack of knowing what the other team was trying to do.

"I was focused on understanding what the game was all about, focused on what the object of the game was. I think it took me two or three years in the pros to really understand what the game was all about. I'm not just talking about catching a ball, blocking, or delivering a good tackle. It's a combination of things that includes your preparation, your ability, and your instinct.

"For example, you just can't teach a defensive back many of the things he has to know and do in order to make an interception. If you could teach those things, then you'd have people breaking my interception record, and there's no one even close to being able to do that. It's the instinct, the feel, and the knowledge that you amass through your experience, ability, and the way you think about what you're doing. It's knowing what you're capable of and also knowing what your opponent is capable of.

"My success didn't start when I had the opportunity to play pro football. It started long before that, and there were a complex set of things that contributed to that. Kids probably have their core values set in place by the time they're around twelve years old. For me, it was long before that. A lot of those values get embedded through osmosis. Kids pick up all kinds of things from what they see...how the parents live, how they talk, what they do, and a million other moments that kids get exposed to. I was fortunate to have parents who instilled strong moral foundations in me at an early age, and that has a lot to do with who I am and what I've accomplished. The way I was raised served as my compass in life.

"I serve as a county commissioner where I live, and the biggest problems we have are on the human service side of things. I think a lot of those problems all come down to a lack of respect. It seems like many people today just don't have respect for other people's feelings. Many people are too interested in themselves and concerned with what they can get or what they can do, without any regard for how their actions might impact other people. I think that's one of the reasons that so many people are getting in trouble today.

"Times have changed since I was a kid growing up in the 1950s. If we did something wrong, the bad news usually beat us home, and our parents knew about it. The people in our neighborhood usually took care of the problem on the spot, when it happened. The people in our neighborhood didn't give you a thirty-minute time out. You usually got a smack across the rear end.

"Today, it's just not like that anymore. You hear about a parent spanking their kid in the grocery store today, and then all of sudden the cops are after them for child abuse. I'm certainly not advocating abusing or hurting kids, but the reality of the situation is that you have to discipline your kids when they do something wrong. If you don't correct those unacceptable behaviors, kids will just keep doing them. You know, the Bible says, *Spare the rod, spoil the kid.* That's all there is to it.

"As far as any advice I might have for parents, I would tell them to encourage their kids to keep trying to the best of their ability. Just never give up. If the kids aren't good enough at something, encourage them to practice more at it. I'd also encourage parents to teach their kids respect. You have to respect other people's opinions and feelings. You just can't get along with others if you don't show them respect."

* * *

At any given moment, you're just who you are, nothing more and nothing less than all the moments that have come to pass up to the present point. But for some folks, just being what they are begs the question of what they might become.

There's a line of delineation between people who achieve success and people who don't. Successful people understand that the past doesn't necessarily dictate what their futures will look like. They understand that they have an option at any given moment to make a decision to embark on a new course of success and accomplishment.

Of course, the moments that make up your life have a tremendous influence upon how you view the world and the circumstances around you. If you have great parents, great teachers, and great influences around you as you develop, your chances at success are dramatically improved. But even if your early development isn't as optimal as it could have been, you've still got the option of making a decision about what kind of outcomes you'd like to see in your life.

We've all heard the saying that the only constant in life is change. Our circumstances constantly change. They are in a constant state of motion, and you're either moving forward or you're moving backwards. There's no sitting still because life is motion, and how you engage in that dance determines the level of success and satisfaction you'll have in your life.

Paul Krause provides the perfect example of "life as motion." His life was full of the active pursuit of the moments that defined him. As a kid, he and his buddies frequently defined themselves through the motion of the various sports they played. As a high school and collegiate athlete, it was his ability to put into motion the skills that he possessed to become a standout athlete. And, as a pro, physically and mentally, he was always anticipating and moving to where the ball was going to be. Perhaps that's why he holds the record for the most interceptions in professional football. He was simply who he was because he capitalized on his moments and maintained his momentum.

Chapter 13

HOWIE LONG

Troubles are often the tools by which
God fashions us for better things.
— Henry Ward Beecher

oward Michael "Howie" Long was born January 6, 1960, in Somerville, Massachusetts. He attended Milford High School in Milford, Massachusetts, and is a member of the Milford Hall of Fame. He played college football at Villanova and capped his collegiate career off by being selected as the MVP in the 1980 Blue-Gray Game. He also boxed at Villanova and was the Northern Collegiate boxing champion.

In 1981 Howie was drafted by the Oakland Raiders in the second round and played for the Oakland/Los Angeles Raiders for thirteen seasons as a defensive end. During his professional career, Howie earned a trip to eight Pro Bowls, was selected as All-Pro in 1983, 1984, and 1985, was NFL defensive player of the year in 1985, was awarded the NFL Alumni Defensive Lineman of the year in 1984 and 1985, was selected first or second team All-AFC Team 1983-1986 and 1989-1990, Super Bowl win in 1984, and inducted into the Pro Football Hall of Fame in 2000.

Howie Long has been married since 1982 to the former Diane Addonizio, and they have three sons and reside in Charlottesville, Virginia. Howie has appeared in several major motion pictures, as well as numerous TV shows and commercials. Today, he's best known as an analyst for the FOX Network's NFL coverage, where he often plays the 'straight guy' to the antics of co-host Terry Bradshaw.

66 **I** didn't have what you'd call the most stable childhood. The neighborhood I grew up in was kind of an infamous neighborhood made up of Italian and Irish Catholics. I grew up right by the Navy yard. It was a low-to-middle class neighborhood, depending upon what street you lived on. It was famous at that time for car thieves and bank robbers.

"I lived with my parents till I was nine, then I ended up living with my grandmother and an uncle in Charlestown, Mass. When I was about fourteen, because of the bussing riots of the mid-'70s, my grandmother decided to send me out to live with another uncle who had kind of lived the American dream and made it to the suburbs. I was the kind of kid who had a great deal of self-doubt, and I think a lot of that was a by-product of my environment.

"We played a lot of games in the street when I was a kid. I lived on a dead end street with the cars parked halfway up on the curb because the streets were so narrow. We played everything there.

"I hadn't participated in any youth sports until I was fourteen. That was just by happenstance during the first day at my new school. A gentleman by the name of Dick Corbin, who was the high school football coach at Milford High School, saw me walking down the hallway and inquired as to who I was, obviously because I had some size. He wanted to know if I had ever played football before. I said, Sure! Being a city kid, you become kind of a chameleon, and I said, Oh yeah, I've played. I didn't know how to play a lick. Didn't even know how to put the equipment on.

"In reality, the real identity of who I am, and my life, started that day in the hallway. It gave me, someone who lacked confidence, a sense of belonging. I had been kind of going from place to place and wasn't really equipped to handle the environment that I was thrust into from a social or economic standpoint. Milford was a middle class kind of area. Being a city kid of limited resources, it was a struggle to fit in.

"That day in the hall was almost like a life preserver being thrown to me in the water. Without exaggeration, it was the turning point in my life. It gave me such a strong sense of self-worth. It gave me a strong concept of we vs. me. It gave me a strong sense of what work was, the commitment that was required, setting goals from an individual and team standpoint. Our team won two state championships the three years I was there.

"Growing up in the Boston area, Bobby Orr was my hero. I grew up wanting to be like Bobby Orr. In fact, I lived and breathed Bobby Orr. I grew up close to the Boston Garden and a lot of the Celtics and Red Sox players were significant role models for me, too. Those were kinds of guys I admired—Bobby Orr, Phil Esposito, Collier Strumsky, Johnny Busik, Jerry Tevers, and Kenny Hodge. When I lived with my Aunt Edie, she had a TV in the kitchen. I was glued two feet away from it, living and dying with every game.

"My grandmother, Elizabeth Mohen, was by far my strongest moral role model. For some reason, she just felt that I was going to be something special, for whatever reason. Lord knows I couldn't see it. She would tell me, *You're going to be something special. You watch.* And this was before I ever played any sport.

"She had a special philosophy about life. She was a devout Catholic and believed that everyone was created equal and that everyone should be treated well. I wasn't raised to see color. Many of the life lessons I got from her I've tried to instill in my children.

"I was probably two-thirds of the way through my senior year of high school before the reality hit me that there might be some athletic opportunity available to me beyond high school. Very few schools recruited me. I ended up signing with Boston College, but the day after I signed, they wanted to move me to offensive line. I played some offensive line in high school, but I felt like I was more of a defensive player. I was familiar with defense, and I lacked confidence in the offensive position. So, I called Villanova and ended up signing with them. It was really then, with about one-third of a term of high school left that some people were telling me there's a chance I could get a scholarship. I never really viewed that as being a reality. I think when you've had so many things pulled out from under you as a kid, you tend not to believe things until they're right in front of you.

"Villanova, being more of an academic school, didn't really challenge me at the athletic levels of a major conference college. When I got to pro football it was really a shock for me. I had a defensive line coach with the Raiders by the name of Earl Legget, as a matter of fact; he was my inductor into the Hall of Fame. Earl was like a second father for me in many ways—not just from a football standpoint, but also from a life standpoint...how you treat people, how you handle your money, how important family is, how important your children are, and how much hard work is required to be great.

"When I went to the Oakland Raiders, I had Art Shell and Gene Upshaw lined up across from me, and they knew every trick in the book. They'd get you going one way, club you, and you'd fall on your face. It was just brutal. Earl said to me, *If you do what I tell you to do and you work as hard as you possibly can, I'll make you wealthy beyond your wildest dreams. I'll make you a household name in every home in America.* And I looked at him thinking this guy from Mississippi must be on crack or something!

"What he did for me was take me to a place physically that I had no idea I could go. I'm talking in terms of preparation, not in terms of playing. The training camps, the practices, and the off-season stuff— it was brutal. After what I went through as a football player, the commitment that I had to make physically and mentally, everything else in life was easy. I think that's one of the great things you get from athletics. The sheer requirements of the preparation that goes into being an athlete, physically and mentally, makes everything else in life seem easy.

"As far as my values are concerned, I would think that they, in terms of how I treated people, were for the most part in place by the time I was an adolescent. From a work ethic and confidence standpoint, all of that came as a by-product of athletics. When I pull in my driveway, I realize that everything I have can be attributed to football.

"The reason I was able to achieve the athletic levels that I have all comes down to this: Who's going to outwork who? I look at some of the young pro defensive linemen, and they have no technique, no idea of how to prepare, no idea how to watch films or how to do the things that they need to be doing. I played with a number of guys who had more ability than I did. I was going to outwork those guys and squeeze every ounce of what I had out of my ability as a football player, mentally and physically.

"I'm sure some of this comes from my socioeconomic background. First, I had nowhere else to go. Second, I was fortunate to have someone like Earl Legget to instill in me a work ethic and a preparation mode that was second to none. I always felt that I was as physically prepared as anyone in the league.

"I grew up in a tough neighborhood, and I wasn't a tough kid. I've told that to my kids, and they think I'm kidding them. It didn't hit me till I was around thirteen years old, and I knocked down my first kid. It dawns on you, sort of like an epiphany, that suddenly you don't have to take this anymore. I was a frightened kid who was just trying to make it day to day, literally. I kind of plotted my way to school and plotted my way home to avoid trouble. That's just where I was at that time, surviving day to day.

"I don't think that there's really any one thing or piece of advice that anyone gave me that made me who I am. I kind of view it as a compilation of things that, if you take collectively, are the building blocks of who you are, who you've become and who you'll become. I'm still working on that.

"When I used to play, I'd go to bed every night and visualize playing every conceivable blocking combination. Now, I go to bed, and I go over my day with the kids and cringe at my shortcomings. Raising kids has been one of the hardest jobs I've ever had.

"One of the biggest things I've had to overcome in my life is that athletics is not the only way that my kids can make it in life. Unfortunately, for my kids, they're under a different microscope than I was. The expectations for them are so much higher. Every time my son walks on the football field, regardless of what number he's wearing, many people have a preconceived notion of what he's supposed to be or there's some kind of misplaced envy or jealousy, or whatever. There are also a lot of good people, but you get a combination of it.

"It's difficult to realize that your child's abilities as an athlete are not a reflection of what they are as a person. And they're not a reflection of you. The thing I'm most proud of about my oldest boy is that he's an independent thinker. He's kind to all the kids on the team, the weaker ones and the stronger ones. His barometer for judging people isn't predicated on their ability as players. What defines your kids is more than what they accomplish athletically.

"To get to where one can get, and where I got in professional sports, you're naturally a competitive person. Not everyone has that. And that's okay. There's nothing wrong with that. What defines your child and what defines you as an individual is not what you do athletically. It's okay not to be great in sports, and I have to remind myself of that sometimes. It was my way of making it, but it may not necessarily be your kid's way. Your kids aren't you.

"It's funny; I played thirteen years in the NFL. I'm in the Hall of Fame, I've been a world champion, I'm on TV, and everything else. But at the end of the day, what did I accomplish? I hit people for thirteen years, and now I talk about hitting people on TV. In the big scheme of things, what am I doing to change the world, even within my little cubical of the world? Funding kids programs, building a Little League field or whatever. Doing things like that are the things I value and enjoy so much."

* * *

Rarely do we get the opportunity to choose our particular circumstance. We don't have our choice of parents. We don't get to pick and choose our God-given talents, and we can't control the actions of some stranger who has just run a stop sign and is headed straight for us. In a sense, we're all just one circumstance away from victory or defeat, from pleasure or pain.

But the reality of circumstance is that we all get our share of it, good and bad, and it's how we choose to react to our circumstance that determines whether or not our particular situations ultimately end up being positive or negative. What might seem like a burden to some may be seen as an opportunity by others, and perhaps that is the defining point between success and failure in any endeavor.

One of the lines in a Robert Frost poem, *The Road Not Taken,* exclaims "how way leads on to way." We make a choice to move in a certain direction, to go a particular *way.* Our path, our *way,* gives rise to countless other *ways* we encounter along our journey, and the quality of the *way* is always contingent upon the earlier choices and experiences one has had along the *way.*

As a kid, Howie Long didn't seem to be on his *way* to any kind of promising future, much less the future of a football star, movie star, and sports announcer. But things happened along his *way,* where two roads diverged, and he took the one that made all the difference.

Chapter 14

ANTHONY MUÑOZ

God gave us two ends—one to sit on and one to think with.
Success depends on which end you use. Heads you win, tails you lose.
— **Unknown**

Michael Anthony Muñoz was born on August 9, 1958. He attended Chaffey High School in Ontario, California, where he played baseball, basketball, and football. As a youth, he was barred from Pop Warner football because he was too big.

Muñoz earned a football scholarship to the University of Southern California, where he received a degree in business. While at Southern California, he was a two-time All American.

He began his professional football career with the Cincinnati Bengals in 1980 and played with Cincinnati until 1992. In 1993 he signed with the Tampa Bay Buccaneers, but injured his knee in the preseason and never played again. Many experts agree that Muñoz was the greatest offensive lineman to ever play professional football. But he was also a talented receiver, compiling seven receptions and four touchdowns as a tackle-eligible receiver for the Bengals.

Muñoz was the third pick in the first round of the NFL Draft in 1980, even though he had some significant knee problems, which limited him to only eight games in his junior and senior year in college.

66 I was born in San Bernidino, California, and grew up in Ontario, California. I've got two older brothers and two younger sisters. I was raised by a single parent. My mom raised five of us by

herself. She worked a couple of jobs to provide for us and took different jobs whenever she could. I didn't know my dad. But the good thing about it was that my mom had four brothers and four sisters. The uncles were there for encouragement and support that I didn't have from my father, like rides to the ball games, or maybe just taking me to dinner or the store to buy me a pair of pants. I had support with other family members. I look at that as being a significant part of growing up without a dad.

"I basically started out playing sports with my two older brothers. My older brother was the one who was teaching me how to play baseball, and that was kind of a mentoring experience. On the other hand, when we would get out in the yard and play we'd be very competitive. We had that sibling rivalry type of thing, but my brothers also took the time to teach me the game, apart from the competitive side.

"I was about six years old when I started my first organized sport, baseball. You had to be nine years old to play in this league, so I had them believing I was old enough to play. My two older brothers were baseball players, and that was my childhood dream—to be a professional baseball player. I wanted to be like them because they were playing. I was the batboy for their teams. My brothers, Tom and Joe, were the biggest influence I had to play.

"Because my mom had to work so much, there were a lot of things we had to do for ourselves. But the thing she always did when I was growing up was attend every one of my Little League baseball games and all my school events. She did the same with all the other kids, too. We didn't have a car, so we had to find ways to get to the games with relatives until my older brother got a car and provided us with rides. My mom supported and encouraged me through my athletic participation.

"Nobody ever forced me to play any particular sport. It was always my decision. That was the one thing that really made me love the sports I was playing. It was my choice. When I got to high school, I played football, basketball, and baseball and nobody told me I had to do this or that sport. I even played one year of baseball at USC when I went to college.

"Outside of my family, I guess there were three people who were role models for me. When I was six, I met a gentleman named Jim

Seamen, who would eventually be my high school baseball coach. He was the head of parks and recreations and I knew that he had played at USC on the '61 National Championship baseball team. He was the one who brought us along and provided new gloves for us and took us to tournaments. He was kind of like a father image for me. Because I was a baseball player as a kid, Brooks Robinson and Warren Mercer were also role models I tried to emulate. I always needed to watch them to see how they were doing.

"My earliest role models were my brothers. They would take me along with them even though I was two and eight years younger than them. My oldest brother taught me how to catch a short hop without turning my head. A lot of tears did I shed in the front yard, but I learned how to get down on the ball and look it into my glove. Most kids will turn their head. He just kept firing them at me. It was tough, but I learned.

"They also taught me to just go out and do my job. Do the job and you don't have to say a whole lot when you're playing, because your play is going to speak louder than your words, and you don't have to chatter and talk and do all that stuff people do. I learned some valuable things from my brothers that I took through high school, college and then my NFL career.

"I was the type of kid who always tried to be polite to people and treat people with respect. When I got to college, I'd have to say my faith is what really took over and became my moral, ethical, and spiritual guidance. That was when I trusted Christ, and that's been my barometer to the present day.

"I was fortunate to have the types of coaches who were disciplined and structured, who believed in doing things the right way, and I was always around those types of coaches. They made sure we didn't embarrass ourselves, or them, and didn't act in an unruly way outside of the field.

"My coaches led by example. Ray Start, my head football coach, was an intense, do-it-by-the-rules type of guy. Always working hard. I wasn't involved with coaches who made the Lombardi speeches or the kind of speeches designed to fire you up. It was through the preparation that we had during the week that would set the table.

"The preparation during the week got you to the peak point when you came to a game. There didn't need to be anything said. It was done by example and preparation, and if you did that well enough, you were going to go out onto the field and just go nuts and prevail. None of the coaches I had were great motivational speakers. It was more like, *Okay, we're here, we're going to get ready, we're going to do this, and we're going to do that. At game time you're going to be ready because I prepared you, and you prepared yourself.*

"If you have the physical gifts, a lot of times you can get by with just being there and doing very little, while perhaps still believing that you're committed and hard working. During my sophomore year at USC I realized I better be in the weight room and running more if I wanted to be competitive in practice. Plus, if I didn't do that, with the kind of competition we had, I'd be kind of left behind in the pack.

"I might look at myself and say I wasn't bad, but I wasn't good enough. As much confidence as I thought I had in my ability, it's interesting to note that my confidence just skyrocketed when I started to notice I'm getting stronger, quicker, and in better shape. A lot of things started to build along with the physical commitment of working out, which excited me. I believe it took me to another level.

"A couple of teammates I had at USC, Brad Buddy and Chris Foote, really taught me what work ethic was all about. These guys looked like they had been in the weight room since they were in kindergarten. They showed me what working hard and being dedicated meant. Not only were they great football players, they also took that dedication into the weight room and their conditioning. That was a critical point in my life. These guys taught me what it meant to be committed in that area and really bust it but still have fun doing it.

"In describing some of the most important traits I had that allowed me to achieve what I've achieved, I think probably the words commitment, loyalty, and accountability fit the best. I think those are skills that you develop and have to build over time. They're habits that you continually have to work on every day. I don't believe I was born with those things. I think those are things that you have to work on, on a daily basis. I worked on those things and wanted to implement them into my play. I wanted the guy next to me to know that I was committed to being the best, committed to him, loyal to him, accountable to him, and that carries over for me into life. Now that I'm retired from football, that's the emphasis in my life, and I try to live that.

"As far as value systems are concerned, I would tend to agree that core values are in place at a pretty early age. We've got two kids in college now, and looking at them and looking back at my life, I think that you also develop these core values to a certain extent. I think you either work on them as you get older, or you don't continue to progress in those areas.

"Support and encouragement would be the best advice I would give to parents of young athletes. That's what we did with our two kids. We told them at an early age that just because your dad played in the NFL, don't feel you have to be in sports. But whatever you do, give it everything you have. If you want to play football, if you want to play soccer, whatever, give it all you've got and have fun. I think you don't pressure kids into a sport, but if they want to play, give them all the support and encouragement you can. Don't make decisions for them because they're the ones who are going to have to go through it. We've taught our kids to make their own decisions along the way as they were growing up. You have to respect those decisions and encourage and support them."

* * *

If it were but a simple task to define success, many more people would rise to the ranks of greatness. But it is no simple task. On the athletic side, success is a complex dance that requires the optimization and coordination of your physical and mental capabilities.

Physically, one must reach beyond what others are willing to do to perform better than their opponent. And it's not just the amount of work you do that makes the difference. It's the focus and intent you have while you're engaged in your preparation. You can run twice as many drills as your opponent, but if you're not running those drills with the focused intent you need to maximize your efforts, the results won't produce the outcomes you were trying to achieve. Your expectations will not be met without focused, deliberate preparation.

Given similar physical abilities, it's the mental component that becomes the difference-maker for success. The mind sees what it expects to see. What gets programmed into the mind, and how you process that information, serves as the basis for the outward manifestation of what you think. It serves as the nucleus of what your eventual action will turn out to be, just like a snowball rolling down a hill. Where you end up depends upon what part of the hill you roll down. You can pick an optimal path to an optimal destination or you can start the process of 'snowball accumulation' with no sense of destination and wind up hitting the tree in the middle of the hill, with no more gained than what you had when you started. If you don't aim, you'll likely not hit your target.

Many experts today contend that natural talent is not the key to success. According to K. Anders Ericcson, the key to success is *deliberate practice.* Deliberate practice is designed to stretch people beyond their current capabilities and consists of high repetition activity, where feedbacks are continually available. It's hard work that requires intense focus and concentration, where you set specific achievement goals, think about how you're thinking about what you're doing, and constantly self-evaluating the activity you're engaged in, so you can continue this process with the intention of improving those things you're not as good at.

The most talented people in any field have combined the characteristics of deliberate practice to achieve success. Positive family environment plays an important role in helping to develop the critical thought processes that helps enable a child to tap into higher human potentials, as do good coaches, good teachers, and good peer groups.

Anthony Muñoz certainly had many of those supporting systems around him, such as his mother, brothers, relatives, coaches, and peers. But at the end of the day, Anthony Muñoz had to combine the complex tapestry of success in his own person, in his own way, and make a choice as to whether he was going to be average or above average. He certainly didn't choose the path of least resistance, and that's apparent in what he has accomplished and in what he continues to accomplish in life today.

Chapter 15

OZZIE NEWSOME

*There's no scarcity of opportunity to make a living at what
you love. There is only a scarcity of resolve to make it happen.*
— **Wayne Dyer**

O zzie Newsome Jr. was born on March 16, 1956, in Muscle
Shoals, Alabama. He was the third of five children. Ozzie
attended Colbert County High School where he was one of
the first African Americans to attend an integrated high school.

Ozzie played college football at the University of Alabama where
he was a starter all four years. He made the College Football All-
American Team in 1977 and assisted the Crimson Tide to a 42-5 overall record during his four seasons. Newsome averaged 20.3 yards per
catch, which was a Southeastern Conference record. He was named
the Player of the Decade for the 1970s and was enshrined in the College Football Hall of Fame in 1994.

"The Wizard of Oz," as he was called, was the twenty-third pick in
the 1978 draft for the Cleveland Browns. He played for the Browns
from 1978 to 1990. In his rookie year, he was named the Browns'
Offensive Player of the Year, the first rookie in twenty-five years to
accomplish that feat. The following year he earned All-Pro honors. He
was also All-Pro in 1984 and was selected three times to participate
in the Pro Bowl.

Ozzie had 662 receptions for a total of 7,980 yards, both franchise
records, and forty-seven touchdowns during his career. In 1986, he won
the Ed Block Award for playing with injuries, and in 1990 he won the
NFL Players Association Whizzer White Award for community service.

Newsome played in 198 consecutive games and caught at least one pass in 150 consecutive games, which was the second longest streak at the time of his retirement. In 1999, he was inducted into the Pro Football Hall of Fame.

After retirement from football, Newsome assumed the role of vice president of player personnel for the Baltimore Ravens. In 2002 he was named the general manager for the Ravens and became the first African-American to occupy that position in the NFL. He is well respected around the league and is considered to be one of the best general managers in professional football.

"I was born in Muscle Shoals, Alabama. I've got two brothers and two sisters, one each older, and one each younger. I'm right in the middle. My mom was a domestic home worker, and my dad owned a restaurant. We lived in the same place my entire childhood.

"All of my siblings were involved in some kind of athletic activity, cheerleading or playing some kind of ball. My older brother was quite a bit older than me, but my younger brother was only a year younger, and we were pretty competitive. He and I were always on opposite sides in all of our sandlot games and activities.

"We lived in a rural setting. There were about fifteen houses around us, and there were always different kinds of games going on—pickup football games, baseball, basketball, and other games.

"My older brother was twelve years older than me, and he was a very good athlete. I would follow him around to watch him play high school sports and summer league baseball, and I think that had a lot to do with my interest in sports. He would teach me how to catch, how to throw a curve ball, and how to shoot a jump shot. He was a big influence on me. And I watched sports on television, too. So, in general, that was something I had an interest in.

"The first organized sport I participated in was the sixth grade basketball team. I was only in the fourth grade when I started playing on the sixth grade team. From there I started playing senior Little League baseball and junior high football and basketball, which was when I was in the eighth grade.

"My parents knew that sports was something I really enjoyed, and they were very supportive from the athletic standpoint. They were always there to pick me up from practice and so forth. They never tried to persuade me not to play sports, and they came to a lot of the games I played. They allowed me the freedom to participate in the sports that interested me, and I played baseball, basketball, and football.

"My mom would have been my primary ethical role model. She taught us about respect—respect for our elders, for other people, and for other peoples' property. My high school coach had an impact on my development as a player and as a person, too.

"My coach was very encouraging. He was very demanding, too. He was the first one to really push my leadership button. He was the one who told me that I needed to be out front and be a leader. He helped me enhance my athletic skills, my leadership abilities, and he insisted that we keep up with our academics and get good grades.

"He was a great influence in my development, but another important aspect of my character was simply the fact that athletics kept me busy and kept me from having too much idle time on my hands. While some other kids might be hanging out with nothing constructive to do, I spent my time athletically. I guess you might say it was my hobby. I just didn't have the extra time to be doing negative things and getting into trouble.

"I got a lot from my athletic experience. I got to meet and experience many different people, which was kind of unique because I grew up in the South during the civil rights era. Athletics was an area that helped cross the racism line, and on the field we were all pretty much the same. It didn't matter what color you were, the best kid was going to be the starter. It also allowed me the opportunity to travel and see other parts of the country. Playing Little League baseball, football, and basketball allowed me to visit other areas and regions. That expanded my universe and allowed me to experience other people.

"Athletics definitely helped me develop my work ethic. It helped me understand that if you want to improve at something, you have to work at it. I was on some high school state championship teams and some undefeated junior high teams. Winning was an important thing that I learned, and a big part of that winning attitude was learning about being a team player and playing as a team.

"There is no question in my mind that athletics, if I had to choose only one thing, was the thing that was most responsible for creating the person I am today. That's where I spent the majority of my time and my focus. Athletics helped me reveal the core values that I learned as a child, and those values were certainly expanded through my athletic exposure.

"As far as my success as an athlete is concerned, it's obvious that you have to have a certain degree of ability to start with. There were people who were bigger and faster than me, but I think I was able to exhibit a consistency with what I did. I was consistent in my athletic activities and in my academic activities. I think I developed that because people around me demanded that kind of thing from me. They demanded that I live with a degree of integrity, and they didn't let me deviate from that.

"I understood that I had some God-given abilities. I was appreciative of those abilities and always had a drive to enhance those abilities. A lot of people might be satisfied with what they've been able to accomplish. Whenever I reached a certain goal, I was always thinking about the next goal I wanted to reach. I wouldn't say I was ever totally satisfied with what I had accomplished on the field, because you always knew there was a higher level above whatever you had done, so you were always focusing on improving upon what you had previously done.

"I frequently tell parents that I believe it's important to expose their kids to sports because I think there are so many lessons—life long lessons—that can be learned from competing in sports. Whether it's individual sports like golf or tennis, or team sports like football and baseball, a person receives so many valuable lessons from sports that positively translate into virtually every aspect of life.

"I never tried to push my own kids into playing a specific sport, and I think that's probably one of the worst things a parent can do. Sure, you should be supportive and enthusiastic about their participation, but the more important thing for a young kid is to enjoy his or her athletic experience. Whatever my own kids participated in, the big thing I tried to impress upon them was to not give up. Enjoy yourself, but don't ever let anybody make you quit. That just sets the stage to make it easier to quit the next time a challenge comes up in their life."

* * *

In the study of human physiology (the study of the function of the body) the first concept you learn is the concept of "use it-or-lose it." Basically, that means if you don't use a body part, you'll eventually lose the function of that part.

Inversely, if one uses a body part more frequently, then that body part will function even more efficiently. To take it a step further, if you really use your parts at higher levels, you get to experience a level of mastery with the function of those parts.

In the case of Ozzie Newsome, it's evident that he found a way to master his abilities and rise to a level of excellence in his performance. And an interesting thing to note is that many experts today wouldn't credit raw athletic ability with the success of someone like Ozzie. What gets the credit is a complex series of exposures that Ozzie had over his lifetime, and how he viewed, processed, and acted on those exposures.

Becoming a master at what you're doing doesn't happen in a few days, weeks, or even months. It's an incremental process that requires the completion of certain developmental stages, which set the stage for advancement to the next higher stage of performance. It's a web, a Pro-matrix™, of interconnected exposures and reactions to those exposures. It's more of a journey than a destination, and you can't miss any of the steps if you want to master your activity.

While Ozzie Newsome was an extremely gifted athlete, his great career is more a result of what he did with his ability than the mere possession of such ability. What he made look extremely easy to do was the result of tremendous dedication and commitment. He was a master at football and is a master at his vocation today. That's why they call him the "Wizard of Oz."

Chapter 16

MERLIN OLSEN

Our greatest glory is not in never failing,
but in rising up every time we fail.
— Ralph Waldo Emerson

Merlin Jay Olsen was born on September 15, 1940, to Lynn Jay and Merle Olsen in Logan, Utah. After attending Logan High School, he accepted an athletic scholarship to Utah State University where he was a member of the Sigma Chi and Phi Beta Kappa fraternities.

At Utah State, Olsen played defensive tackle. As a senior, he was a consensus All-American and was the winner of the Outland trophy (best college interior lineman). He was All-Conference in 1960 and 1961 and was an Academic All-American in 1961. As a senior at Utah State, Olsen's team only gave up an average of 50.8 rushing yards per game, which led the nation at that time and still stands as a school record for defense. Not known as a national power football program, the Utah State Aggies finished tenth in the AP and UPI polls during Olsen's senior year, the only time in the history of the program they've been ranked that high.

Olsen played in the East-West Shrine Game in 1961 and in 2003 was voted to that game's Hall of Fame. He played in the Hula Bowl and was voted MVP of the game. He's a member of the State of Utah's Sports Hall of Fame, the Utah State University Sports Hall of Fame, and the university's All-Century Team. In 2000 he was selected by *Sports Illustrated* as one of Utah's Top 50 Athletes of the Century, and he was voted to the All-Academic All-American Hall of Fame in 1988.

Olsen was drafted by the Los Angeles Rams in 1962. He was the third pick in the first round of the draft. He played for Los Angeles from 1962 to 1976 and missed only two games during his fifteen-year career. He was part of one of the best front fours in NFL history. Deacon Jones, Rosey Grier, and Lamar Lundy joined Olsen on the defensive line that was nicknamed the "Fearsome Foursome." Olsen was named to fourteen Pro Bowls, the most for any player in history. He was selected for the NFL 75th Anniversary All-Time Team, the 1970s NFL All-Decade Team, the 1960s NFL All-Decade Team, the Bert Bell Award in 1974, and was the Pro Bowl MVP in 1968. He was named to the College Football Hall of Fame in 1982, the High School Hall of Fame in 1987, and the Pro Football Hall of Fame in 1982, along with numerous other awards and recognitions.

After professional sports, Olsen was a football commentator with NBC through the 1980s. He also enjoyed success as an actor, most notably with Michael Landon in *Little House on the Prairie* and as the lead actor in the series *Father Murphy* and *Aaron's Way*. He's the national spokesman for the National Association for the Self-Employed and is a motivational speaker for many *Fortune* 500 companies. He resides in Salt Lake City, Utah, and does many community and fund-raising projects for charities.

66 **I** was born in northern Utah in a town called Logan. I grew up there and went to school there. I'm the second oldest of nine children. My father was a soil scientist. He worked for the Bureau of Reclamation. My mom pretty much had her hands full taking care of us kids.

"Things were always busy around our house. Growing up, initially we had two bedrooms and one bathroom until we eventually expanded the house. There was competition between the kids, but being the oldest boy, I didn't have that much of a sense of competition with my younger siblings. I think they felt more of that than I did.

"Our house was right across the street from the park—Central Park—

which had some real advantages for us. In the summertime I was always outside either chasing up and down the hillsides or fishing up in the canyons or riding my bike somewhere. In the winter, I would ice skate all the time at the park. I'd come home from school, put on my ice skates, and skate till I got tired. I ice-skated so much that I developed very powerful legs, which I think helped in my football career.

"I always loved sports and activities of any kind. It didn't matter what it was. But the difficult thing for me was that I was uncoordinated in my earlier days. I'd fall down walking on a flat sidewalk! I was always the last one chosen for football games or other teams at Central Park. It almost got to be a joke, because it was such an important thing to me. I really wanted to be an athlete. I wanted to be a part of the team. I wanted to be out there, but I was growing so fast that I was uncoordinated all the way through the ninth grade. It's a funny irony that they've since renamed the old park we used to play in Merlin Olsen Park.

"I went out for everything. But I never made a single team of any kind, except the ones where they had to take you. I was cut from the basketball and football teams in the eighth and ninth grade. I had very little success—almost no success at all, until I went to high school. In fact, I've talked to my ninth grade coach since then about not making the team. He told me that he should have probably seen the potential. I told him if I had been in his place, I would have cut me, too, because I wasn't able to do what he needed me to do at that time.

"By the time I was a sophomore in high school, I finally started getting my coordination. I made the JV football squad, and that was exciting for me, because I hadn't made any teams prior to that. I think the best game, or the most exciting game I ever played, was my very first game. We watched the other team get off of the bus, and they had a couple of guys who were over 300 pounds, and they had three times as many players as our team. I remember thinking that we didn't even have a chance against these guys. Well, we beat them so badly that it wasn't even a game, and it was just terribly exciting. I had so much adrenalin pumping, I must have made twenty tackles! It was kind of an awakening for me. It was finally an opportunity to feel like I could succeed at something.

"My parents encouraged me to get out and do things. But by the time I got into high school, they were so busy that they didn't have a chance to see too many of my games. I provided my own impetus to play. It was just something I wanted to do. By the time I got to high school, if there was time in the day to do it, I was going to do it. That not only applied to sports but other activities, too, whether it was a school play, debate, ROTC, or whatever, I was involved in.

"I never felt any pressure from my parents to play or not, but I remember my mom telling me she didn't want me to play football, because she was afraid I would get hurt. I told her there are some things we can talk about and some things we can't, and this is one of the things we can't talk about. She was wise enough to see how important it was to me and she backed off of that.

"We didn't have a TV when I was growing up, so I didn't really have any celebrity athletic role models. I probably couldn't have named six pro teams by the time I was a sophomore in college. I spent a lot of time thinking about sports and I enjoyed going to and watching the high school teams. I would watch the Utah State team, too. I would sneak over the fence or sign up to sell soft drinks at the game. I spent a lot more time watching the game than I did selling drinks.

"My parents were my primary ethical and moral role models, especially as it relates to my work ethic and commitment to family and church. I think you're born with some of your character, and I think you absorb some of it from your environment, too. Whichever may be the case, I think you can strengthen that character. It's a cyclical type of thing. Once you begin to better understand it and start achieving some level of success, the cycle helps you understand that this is something you want to do, and you start preparing yourself and throwing yourself into the task at hand, until finally you're able to see your efforts come to fruition. The cycle becomes easier and easier for you, but getting through it the first time, of course, is the difficult part for most people, especially for youngsters.

"The thing I appreciated most about my coaches was that they were always encouraging. In a small town like I grew up in, we had two coaches and an athletic director. We had two coaches who would handle all the different sports. We had volunteer coaches and some of the teachers would help, but basically two coaches handled everything. It's not like that today, but I didn't feel like it was a disadvantage. Our coaches were really good people, and they were interested in seeing us grow and learn and were excited about our success.

"As a junior in high school I started to better understand that sports could create other opportunities for me. I made the All-State team as a junior, which actually came as quite a surprise to me. I was very excited about that. I was playing football strictly for the love of it and the enjoyment of being out there. As a senior, I began to get more and more recognition. I probably had about 150 scholarship offers by the time I was ready to decide on a college. Because I had almost straight A's in high school, I could qualify at Ivy League schools, elite schools, PAC 10 schools, and others. I had all these kinds of people interested and offering scholarships.

"I didn't understand this whole scholarship process that much. It was exciting to me, but what was important, as far as I was concerned, was that I was going to college anyway, scholarship or not. Had I not played football, I would have still gone to college. That was always my plan. But I was excited about the opportunity to have an athletic scholarship.

"As far as sports no longer being any fun, that was never the case for me. Even as a pro, sports were fun. If it stopped being fun, I would quit playing, and that's just what I did. I even had to convince the owner of the Rams, Carol Rosenbloom, that I wouldn't sign another two-year contract because he was blocking negotiations with the networks and my opportunity to be a commentator. He was so convinced that I was going to stay, he was telling the networks that they couldn't talk to me.

"Even in college, when I had been an All-American for two years, won the Outland Award, and the pro scouts were drooling, I was interviewing with IBM, Xerox, and Union Oil. Plus, the contracts they were offering were within a couple of thousand dollars of what the Rams were offering. I sat down with my wife and asked, What do we want to do? Should we try this football thing or should we just go right to work? We made a conscious decision to play football because we thought it would be fun.

"I think there are probably two words that accurately define why I was able to be successful as an athlete. Commitment would be the first. It took a long time to finally get to where I could be successful at being an athlete, but I was willing to commit to do what I needed to do to get there, to have the skills that would allow me to be successful as an athlete. If someone had told me that I had to practice twenty-four hours a day for three days, I would have done that. That wouldn't have bothered me, because it was important to me. The other thing would be concentration. I was able to generate real concentration on the elements that were essential in preparing me to compete.

"I think my core value systems were in place by the time I was around twelve years old. In fact, I'm sure they were. I think we have to be very careful not to encourage young people to become so entranced with sports that they forget that sports is just one piece of their lives. I think one of the reasons that I've been able to maintain successful competitive activities, not only in sports but in other areas as well, is the fact that I was a well-rounded person.

"I carried that same competitive attitude off the field and into the classroom and into the business world and into the acting and broad-casting field. I wanted to be as good as I could be and was willing to make the commitment to work at being good. If we allow young people to become so entrenched in sports that they forget about the other pieces of life, then we're doing them a great disservice.

"Sports should be fun for kids, and if it's not fun, it doesn't belong. You should eliminate it. When we put kids into a situation where they're practicing and not enjoying what they're doing when they're really young, we're not helping them at all. They need to have time to be a kid.

"There's a time when you get to high school and college where the perspective begins to change some. But for young kids, all too often they have parents telling them not to smile, and to put on their game faces. When you're ten years old, there shouldn't be any game face. It should be fun. It's the responsibility of the parents who are associated with these programs to make sure that the kids are having fun and to make sure that they're all having an opportunity.

"All of my kids competed athletically. Sometimes it was hard to just stand there and not say anything when some of the parents were out of line. I've had a few conversations with some of the coaches off to the side, but I just don't think you need to do those kinds of things in front of the kids. I've had to absolutely bite my tongue on more than one occasion. It just doesn't make any sense to have parents and coaches—acting like they're Vince Lombardi—talking to ten-year-olds demanding better performance out of the kids. It's supposed to be fun."

* * *

You may have heard the story about Thomas Edison in his quest to create a light bulb. After trying thousands of different configurations and materials, he was still unable to create an incandescent light that would work satisfactorily. Upon being confronted about all his failures he replied, "I have not failed. I've just found 9,999 ways that won't work."

To Edison, and others who achieve high accomplishment, failure is merely an opportunity to learn more about how to achieve an end-goal. Failure isn't a step backward—it's an opportunity to advance another step forward. Greatness doesn't dwell on repeating mistakes. Greatness dwells on the pursuit of solutions to unsolved problems.

Edison is a prime example of how events don't define our lives. He could easily have said that there was just no way to create a light bulb. What makes the difference with someone like Edison? It's simply a question of belief. He believed there was a solution to the problem, and he had the resolve and persistence to keep at it until he found the solution.

Everyone is confronted with a myriad of different events in their life, and it's not those events that define who we are. It's the belief we have about what those events mean.

Imagine what it was like for Merlin Olsen as a kid. He was the kid nobody wanted on his team. But Merlin Olsen had an ace-in-the-hole. He believed. He believed he could be part of a team. He believed he could be an athlete. He believed he could be the best person he could be, and all the early setbacks and disappointments weren't going to keep him from achieving his goals. He understood, as Napoleon Hill once said, "Whatever the mind can conceive and believe, it can achieve."

Chapter 17

MEL RENFRO

The starting point of all achievement is desire. Keep this constantly in mind. Weak desire brings weak results, just as a small amount of fire makes a small amount of heat.
— **Napoleon Hill**

Melvin Lacy "Mel" Renfro was born in Houston, Texas, on December 30, 1941. In 1943, his family moved to Portland, Oregon, and Mel attended high school there at Jefferson High School where he's included as a "Notable Alumni" of that school.

Mel attended the University of Oregon and excelled as a track star and as a two-way football player. As a two-time All-American halfback and defensive back, he rushed for 1,532 yards and scored 141 points, leading the team in rushing for three consecutive years. Renfro was also part of a world record-setting 440-yard relay team in 1962 with a time of forty seconds.

Mel was drafted by the Dallas Cowboys in the second round of the 1964 NFL Draft. He only carried the ball a total of six times for the Cowboys, as Head Coach Tom Landry saw Renfro as a defensive back.

Renfro was initially placed as a safety for the Cowboys but was switched to cornerback in his fifth season, and he became an exceptional threat to the wide receivers of opposing teams. In 1969, he led the league in interceptions with ten. He also was a force on special teams, performing punt and kickoff return duties. In 1964, he led the league in kickoff return yardage.

In his fourteen seasons with Dallas, he intercepted fifty-two passes, returning them for 626 yards and three touchdowns. He returned 109 punts for 842 yards and one touchdown; eighty-five kickoffs for 2,246 yards and two touchdowns, and recovered thirteen fumbles.

Renfro was blessed with excellent speed and earned an invitation to the Pro Bowl in his first ten seasons with Dallas. He was an All-NFL choice five times and earned All-Conference honors seven times. He played in four Super Bowls and eight NFC championship games. He became the fifth member of the exclusive Ring of Honor in 1981 and was enshrined in the Pro Football Hall of Fame in 1996.

Since his retirement from professional football, Renfro has committed himself to building up the inner city community through the efforts of the Mel Renfro Foundation, whose mission is "to restore today's youth and family unit back to the basic values that were built on Godly principles through a Christian-based inner city Bridge Community Center."

" I was born in Houston, Texas. When I was about two years old, my family moved to Portland, Oregon. I was the youngest of four boys. After we moved to Oregon, my dad was a janitor for Montgomery Ward, and my mom worked part-time at the shipyard.

"We lived in a project area called Vanport. That's where a lot of black people were moving looking for better jobs and lifestyles than they had in the South. They were just basic, two-story project homes, and I remember there being a tennis court and a park area there.

"We didn't have any tennis rackets, but we skated a lot on the tennis courts and did a lot of running and jumping and just playing like kids do. My dad was a big baseball fan, so we threw the ball around a lot and hit the baseball. After about three years, we bought a house in the inner city of Portland, and I lived there until I went off to college.

"I remember my brothers and I spending a lot of time together. In fact, our whole family spent a lot of time together whenever we could. Church was also a significant part of our family, and we were charter members of the Hughes Memorial Methodist Church in Portland.

"Growing up with three brothers wasn't really competitive. It was more of a teaching and learning environment with my brothers. My oldest brother, Dallas, was a good athlete in track, basketball, and football. We kind of looked up to him, and he would come home and teach us about the sports he was playing. It was a trickle-down effect sort of thing. As soon as one of us was old enough, one of the older brothers would teach us to broad jump, high jump, shoot the basketball, hit the baseball, and things like that.

"My brother Dallas would teach Jimmy, then he would teach Ray, and I would be observing all of this. Having older brothers involved in sports was a good thing to be around as I was growing up, and I'm sure it had a lot to do with my ability, and it helped me to pick things up very quickly. I learned how to ride a bicycle when I was about three and a half years old. So, it wasn't really a competitive environment with my brothers. It was more of us doing things together, learning and building together.

"I was about eight or nine years old when I started playing organized sports. I played in a baseball Little League and played basketball in grade school. The biggest influence to play was my brothers. When I was pretty young, four or five years old, I would see my brothers participating in sports, and it just got in my blood, and sports were a primary focus for me.

"When we moved into our house in a regular neighborhood, there were a lot of parks around there. We spent a great deal of time in the parks. We would throw the ball around, shoot baskets, hop over benches, and generally run around. We were very active and physical.

"My parents always encouraged me. Even as a young child I remember their encouragement, particularly my dad. He was a big baseball fan, and I remember he would try to be at any sports event I participated in. If he could be there, he always would be. And it was the same way with my brothers. They would always try to be at the games, too.

"I remember one time when I was a freshman in high school. My brother Dallas had joined the service, and I didn't even know he was in the country. I had received a punt and was streaking down the sideline for a touchdown, and I looked over to the sideline and there he was, standing in his trench coat. When I saw him there, something just exploded in me because I was just so happy and proud that he was there. He was there for as long as he could be, but had to leave before the game was over. That's just the way our whole family was. Whenever we could be there for one another, we were.

"My parents always encouraged me to do whatever I wanted to do and to give my best effort at whatever I was doing. They never told me to play this-or-that sport. About the only time I remember them ever trying to influence me was when I was deciding which college to go to. They wanted me to go to the University of Oregon, instead of Oregon State. My parents seemed to think that was the best choice for me, so I took their advice and chose the University of Oregon.

"As far as any athletic role models that I had growing up, I remember I always wanted to be like Jim Brown and Lenny Moore. I admired professional sports, but I never thought I'd ever play professional sports until later in my college career. That just didn't seem like a reality to me.

"My parents were my primary role models as far as my character is concerned. But my high school coach was a significant role model, too. He was always there for me and very supportive of me. And it wasn't just me he gave that attention to. He did that with all the players. If I hadn't had a dad, he would have been my dad. He was just a great guy.

"One significant thing he did when I was in high school was to make me the quarterback. Back in those days, to have a black quarterback wasn't something that happened too often. But the coach believed in me. There were a lot of white alumni who didn't particularly care too much for his decision to put me at quarterback. Coach caught a lot of flack from some people, but he told them that I was a great runner and a great leader and that I was the man he was going to stick with. That always impressed me about him.

"My high school coach was a reserved, soft spoken man. And while he didn't always say a whole lot, one thing he said was that football was a sport and a game to be played, and if you're going to play, you've got to have fun while you're doing it. But he also said that you've got to work hard and train to get in shape. He didn't really push us, but he found a way to make all the hard work fun for us. I don't ever remember him yelling at us in high school. It was always the quiet encouragement that got us motivated. He had a special way to get us to be overachievers and enjoy it while we were doing it.

"So, that was a fun time for me. Today, there seems to be so much pressure involved in athletics—by the coaches, the alumni, and the parents. You see too many coaches yelling at players these days. I was fortunate to have a coach who didn't need to do that kind of thing, and we were pretty successful in high school. We won two state championships and only lost one game the whole time I played high school football. That was the last game I played in high school and was for the state championship. We accomplished that without ever hearing our coach yell at us once. He was just a master positive motivator.

"There was a lot of excitement and fun associated with playing high school football. When I started my sophomore year in college, the atmosphere changed. That was the first time I really felt any pressure to perform, and it was like I took a giant leap to an entirely new level. All of a sudden I got thrust into an environment full of media coverage, big crowds, and a lot of attention. That was the first time I really understood that the objective was to win and that I had to perform. Up to that point sports had been just a game to me, and it was pure fun.

"My college coach, Len Casanova, was a great coach and another role model for me. He was a dedicated and hard working coach, but he tended to raise his voice a little bit, and I was a quiet, introverted kid who had never had any contentious pressure put on me. I didn't appreciate the shouting and contentious behavior, but I did respond and always gave my best effort, because that's just the nature of the way I always played.

"Up until my college sophomore year, athletics was just pure fun and excitement. We only lost one football game in high school. We won three state track championships. And even as a college fresh-man, we rolled over everybody we played. I was always on the winning side, and those days just couldn't have been any better. When I hit my sophomore year in college, things went up to another level. And the same thing happened when I went to my first training camp in the pros. I got whacked around a little bit, and the other guys would say, *Welcome to the NFL.* It was an entirely new level, and you had to rise to the occasion or get left by the wayside.

"Coach Tom Landry was another person who had a profound im-pact on me. He was a devout, strong Christian and tried to run his team based on Christian values and principles. It was easy to see that it was tough for him at times, because there was a secular environment on the team that didn't necessarily adhere to the same beliefs that the coach was advocating. I didn't realize it at the time, but Coach Landry was trying to build a foundation for our team and develop the coordination of the team, and he was doing this in a very professional way. He was meticulous and organized, and he demanded that things be done in a certain way.

"The first five years I played for Coach Landry, I didn't like him very much. He was trying to get me to do things that I wasn't accustomed to, and I was having a hard time understanding why he wanted me to do these things. It took me a while to understand, but I finally did. He was building an efficient, coordinated team, and he was giving us life-lessons at the same time. I think he knew that the value side of the equation was equally as important as the talent side, and that if you couldn't get both of those things running on the same track, you weren't maximizing the potentials of the team.

"I remember Coach Landry would tell us not to be concerned about why he was telling us to do something. He would say just be con-cerned with doing what I tell you, and that understanding why wasn't required. The more we adhered to his system, the more we gelled as a team. But we had to do it exactly like he wanted it done, because if one person didn't execute their assignment, the entire system would break down and it wouldn't work.

"I think an outcome from that kind of coaching was that we learned to play together, execute his instructions, and create a winning program. I think we had better sportsmanship on our team than any other team in the league had. We had good relationships with one another as players. Even if some of the guys weren't friends off the field, we always got along on the field, and we played well together. We played as a team, and Coach Landry instilled that into us. His twenty winning seasons was all about the character of the man and his consistency.

"As far as my success is concerned, I think there are two critical things that apply to me. First, my belief in God shaped my character in important ways. I always wanted to do the right thing. Even as a little child I remembered the Ten Commandments and always tried to do the right kinds of things and be the best I could be. As a Christian, I came to understand that was the only way to have real success in life, and my Christian faith is the barometer of who I am and what I do.

"I think the other thing that contributed to my success was just my desire to be good at what I was doing. I always had this innate feeling in me to jump high and run fast. I believe it was His spirit telling me that, *Mel, you can do this, you can be this, and I expect you to do this and be this.* It was just that feeling that I had that helped me rise above all the crap. And with the encouragement of people like my parents, brothers, and coaches, I just excelled at what I was doing.

"By the time I was about six years old my core values were already in place. I realized what was good and bad, what I should and shouldn't do. That had everything to do with my parents and the closeness of our family. Today, it's a little more difficult to have that kind of contact because you've got two parents working, and lifestyles are different today than they were when I was a kid.

"As far as any advice I would give to parents today, I'd encourage them to spend more time together as a family, especially when the kids are younger and growing up. Just create some extra family time and family stuff to do. It doesn't matter what kind of activity it is, it's just important to do stuff together as a family. I think that's just really important. Even when my parents weren't around, I had my brothers around me, and that helped create a strong family bond. That bond is important, and it's the glue that shapes and holds together the character of a kid."

* * *

Achievement always begins with desire, and desire always origi- nates from some thought or image that the mind conceives. But desire alone is not sufficient to produce success in an endeavor. One must also have a strong belief in the desire to succeed, and one must take actions to make that desire a reality.

For example, a ten-year-old boy is participating in organized foot- ball for the first time. He likes the sport, and has a desire to be on the starting team. For whatever reasons, he has a strong belief that he can be a starter and focuses on learning the plays and gives his best effort in practice. He even does extra things off the field, such as running, watching football games, and reading sports magazines to help him better understand the dynamics of the game. Even though he may not be the biggest or fastest kid on the team, he earns the starting spot.

Success could be described as a trilogy. You must have desire. You must have belief. You must take action. One of the interesting things about this particular formula is that the three components tend to feed on one another. When you have a strong desire to do something, and believe you can achieve that, the actions that you take to achieve your goal tend to reinforce and strengthen your desire and belief. And, as your desire and belief are strengthened, you take even greater action toward achieving the goal. It's a feedback loop bound only by the self- limitations one sets.

A couple of detractors that would contribute to a person's inability to successfully implement this formula would include self-image and the fear of failure. Suppose a child was raised in an environment where positive reinforcement was lacking and the parents, or significant others, berated the child and created a self-image of unworthiness.

That child would be at a critical disadvantage to believe that he/she could accomplish something, having been taught that he/she is not worth much anyway.

Likewise, a fear of failure is all too often the pathogen that keeps people from moving forward with an idea or dream. Their fear is so great that it paralyzes their ability to move forward because the prospect of failure is simply more than they can stand to bear. Ironically, successful people fail far more often than unsuccessful people. It's all about how successful people look at failure. They see failure as an opportunity to learn how to do it right the next time.

The environment you grow up in has a significant impact on your success in life. Mel Renfro is a good example of that. He had so many positive inputs, on so many different levels, that it's no surprise that he had the desire, faith, and ability to take action to become one of the greatest football players in history.

Chapter 18

MIKE SINGLETARY

We first make our habits, and then our habits make us.
— John Dryden

Mike Singletary was born in Houston, Texas, on October 9, 1958. After graduating from Evan E. Worthing High School in Houston, he went on to play for Baylor University where he amassed 662 career tackles, and in 1980 was a Lombardi Trophy Finalist. He was the only college junior to be selected to the All-SWC Team of the 1970s, and he earned All-American honors in his junior and senior years.

Singletary was the thirty-eighth pick in the second round of the NFL draft in 1981. He spent his entire twelve-year career as middle linebacker with the Chicago Bears. At 6´0´´ and 230 pounds, Singletary became a starter for the Bears in the seventh game of his rookie season (1981).

During his career in Chicago, Singletary was known as "The Heart of the Defense." He had a no-nonsense approach to the game and earned the nickname *Samurai Mike,* in recognition of the intimidating focus and intensity he displayed on the field. He was also known as the *Minister of Defense,* as he is also an ordained minister.

Singletary appeared in ten Pro Bowls, was selected as the Most Valuable Defensive Player by the AP or UPI five times, was elected to the College Football Hall of Fame in 1995, was All-Pro eight times, and All-NFC every year from 1983 to 1991. He amassed an impressive 1,488 career tackles, seven interceptions, and twelve fumble recoveries, while only missing two games throughout his career. In 1999,

Mike was ranked number 56 on *The Sporting News'* list of the 100 Greatest Football Players. He was elected to the Pro Football Hall of Fame in 1998.

After his professional football career, Singletary became the linebacker's coach for the Baltimore Ravens and is currently the head coach for the San Francisco 49ers. He is also a noted motivational speaker and has authored three books, *Singletary One on One, Calling the Shots,* and *Daddy's Home at Last.* He and his wife, Kim, have seven children.

"I was born in Houston, Texas. I'm the last of ten kids, five brothers and four sisters. My father was a self-employed construction worker and a Pentecostal pastor. He was stern. Sometimes we spent twelve hours in church on Sunday. My mom was basically a housewife. When I was twelve, my mom and dad divorced, and that dysfunction between them created some turmoil in the house. It was kind of abusive by the time I was growing up.

"I grew up in an all-black neighborhood where most people were poor. But they were proud, hard-working people. There were a lot of latchkey kids in the neighborhood, and we played a lot of unorganized sports at the local park. I played football and basketball, and the park had other types of programs to be involved in. When I played in the neighborhood I always felt I did well at the sports I played, so that was just something I started doing. I loved playing football. We played touch football on the streets and tackle football on the grass. The park was actually the lifeblood of the neighborhood. But I'm lucky I ever got to play any organized sports.

"As a Pentecostal pastor, my father thought sports was against the tenets of his faith, and we were not allowed to participate in any sports. None of my brothers or sisters ever got to play any organized sports, and they were more talented than I was. My father basically thought sports was foolishness and a waste of time. And my mom was against it, too, because I had been kind of sickly as a kid. I was in and out of the hospital with all kinds of respiratory problems the first five or six years of my life. I even slept in an oxygen tent sometimes. So, it didn't even make any sense to talk to my mom about playing. She was just against it.

"But I would beg mom and dad to let me play and, for whatever reason, perhaps the grace of God, my dad finally signed the papers to allow me to play. I think he saw it in my eyes that this was my life. I was about twelve when he let me play, and I remember that he made my closest brother go with me to my first game.

"My dad wanted my brother to report back to him to let him know how I did in the game. He had said that if it looked like I could play and I was adding something to the team, then I could keep playing. If I was just sitting on the bench wasting time, then I couldn't play. My dad and my brother didn't understand that this was the varsity team I was playing on. I was only in the seventh grade, but the entire team dressed out with the varsity. I really had no chance of playing. But, as I stood on the sideline, our team was getting killed, and the coach looked over at me and told me to get in the game. We were getting stomped. The game was basically over.

"So, here I was in the game when the biggest fullback I ever saw in my life came through the hole on a trap play. I was playing middle linebacker and, as he came through the hole, I just faded into the crowd, as he jumped me and kept going. I'd love to say my career started with a bang, but it didn't. On the way home I was very quiet because I realized that I didn't do anything to contribute to the team, and I felt like my brother was going to report that back to my dad. But, to my surprise, my brother looked at me and said, *You know what, Mike? Maybe you have something. Those are big guys out there. Maybe you'll do okay. You know what? I'll tell dad you did all right, tell him you did okay.* I don't know what got into my brother because we were always fighting. But he told my dad I did okay, so dad let me play. The rest is history.

"I had two primary athletic role models growing up. One was Roger Staubach of the Dallas Cowboys and the other was Willy Lanier of the Kansas City Chiefs. To me, Staubach exemplified what an ethical,

Christian man should be. Whether they won a game or lost a game, I never saw anybody compete as hard as he did. And when they won, he was the same as when they lost. Like if somebody asked him who the better team was after a game, he would say, *We got beat today. They were the better team.* He always handled himself gracefully, and I admired him for that. As far as ethical role models, my mom would be number one. My pastor, Reverend Perry, was also a wonderful man whom I always saw walk the talk.

"The first coach who really had an impact on me was my track coach in high school, Coach Miller. I was just a little guy trying to figure out who I was and dealing with all the chaos between my mom and dad. Coach Miller came along at a real pivotal point in my life. I didn't know who I was. I was just a small kid trying to figure out where in the heck I was going to go. I had an idea in my mind that I could do good things, even great things, but I just had no opportunity for an open door.

"Coach Miller came in and helped me realize that there was something about me, and he helped me begin to look at myself and my abilities. He started to kind of tease me with my football coach. I was okay at football, but not great, because all the other kids were bigger than me. Coach Miller would kind of negotiate with my football coach (Coach Hudson) and say something like, *Hey, coach, I'll give you a quarter for that kid. I think he's going to be all right. I think a quarter is about enough for him.* Of course, Coach Hudson would say, *Well, I don't' know. A quarter may be a little high. Let me think about it.* So, they would go back and forth like that.

"I can remember the day that Coach Miller said something to me, and he had no idea how much impact it had on me. He said, *Mike, son, I'm going to call you suitcase.* I had low esteem to begin with, so I'm thinking, wait a minute. This guy is making fun of me. I really liked him, and now he's messed that up, too. I asked, Suitcase? Suitcase? Why are you calling me suitcase? This is what he told me: *Son, I want you to understand something. I see something in your eyes, and with that kind of focus, you're going to go places. You're going to go places all over the world. So, you'll be traveling a lot. So, get your bags ready!* I remember him telling me that I would perform in front of many people who would watch me and that whatever I have, whatever gift I have, I would perfect it.

"Even today, I kind of get the chills when I think about it. But, from that day forth, something within me just began to grow, and I just believed what Coach Miller had said. I just began to put everything I had into whatever I was doing. Sometimes Coach Miller would pull me aside and say, *Son, if you want to do something, do it, and do it right. Do it with all your heart. Don't just go out there and go through the motions. There are all kinds of people. I can get anybody to just go through the motions, but I need somebody to go out there and do it with their heart. If I can get you to compete from your heart, then I'm going to get something very special.* So, I began to try to incorporate that into everything I did.

"I was getting positive feedback from the coach every day about something. Whether it was school, class, or on the field, what he talked about all the time was doing it with heart. I think that's the reason he loved track so much, because it's an individual thing, and you can't blame anybody else. It's all about preparation, and if you're willing to prepare, there's no limit to what you can do. That's what I learned from Coach Miller.

"I think I realized that sports could be a great opportunity for me after the first visit from Baylor University. At my high school we didn't have many kids who got scholarships. We were an all-black high school. Our school was very poor—no weight machines, no fancy equipment, no nothing. So, college scouts really didn't come and watch us. I don't remember any of our guys ever getting any scholarships.

"When I got ready to go to high school, I remember begging my mom to let me go across town to play at this other high school where many of the college scouts would go. Of course, my mom, in all her wisdom, said, *If God wants you to play football, son, he's also at the school you're going to. If you're as good as you think you are, they'll find you.* That wasn't what I wanted to hear, and I was very frustrated at that. My mother made me go to the school I didn't want to go to because she said if it was good enough for all my brothers and sisters, it was good enough for me.

"I had heard that I had a chance at getting a scholarship. But, in all honesty, I had no idea what a scholarship really was. I just knew I wanted one because it was supposed to be a great thing. I knew it had something to do with getting a college education, but I thought it was more like an award or something that somebody would give you. I thought you still had to pay for school and do what everybody else had to do to go to college. I just had no concept at that point in my life. None.

"I remember that first time Baylor University came to visit me. The recruiter's name was Ron Barns, and as he walked into the room, with a Southern accent he said, *Hey, Mike Singletary, I want to talk to you about going to Baylor University!* He was a great guy—a great car salesman type. He sat me down and told me that Grant Teaff (Baylor Head Coach) wanted to offer me a full scholarship to Baylor. And I said, Oh, that's great, thank you! But I had no idea what a scholarship really was.

"So, Baylor asked me to come visit the school. I was so naïve, I was wondering if I had to pay for the visit. I'm wondering who's going to drive me there and how are we going to do this. Then I find out Baylor is going to fly me to the university, and I'm scared to death. I've never flown before in my life, and that airplane trip was absolutely the worst flight anybody could have ever had. I was so addled that I even missed the banquet I was supposed to go to.

"At any rate, Ron Barnes is showing me around and, during recruiting weekend, everybody was having fun with parties and other activities. So, Ron asks me what party I want to go to. I told him I didn't want to go to any party. I just want to sit down and talk about Baylor. He said, *Man, are you kidding me? You don't want to go to a party and meet the girls?* I told him that's not what I was here for. My mom had told me not to forget where I had come from and not to forget why I was visiting Baylor. So, I went there and just sat down and talked to him about the University. I walked around campus for a while and went back to my room and prayed and went to bed. But I knew that's where I wanted to go to school.

"The next day I met the head coach, and he asked me if I understood what Baylor was asking me to do. I said I understand that you're offering me a scholarship, and that I was very appreciative of that. I also asked him what exactly a scholarship was? He said, *That means that we're asking you to come play football for our university and that you won't have to pay for anything. You won't have to pay for your books, you won't have to pay for your classes, you won't have to pay for your lodging and you'll get three meals a day.* I said, Oh Man! What? Well, I was beside myself at that point. I didn't even get three meals a day at home! It was just amazing to me that I could come to this dining hall and eat all I wanted three times a day, every day. For me, that was worth as much as anything else associated with the scholarship. I never understood why some of the guys complained about the food and other things. I never once complained about the food. It was excellent!

"When I got back home after my visit to Baylor, I found out that Coach Teaff wasn't even originally looking at me. He was looking at another kid, a running back. Coach Teaff just happened to see me when he was scouting this other kid and ended up saying that he wanted me. That's how I ended up getting a scholarship. And I had other people pulling for me, too. I remember how some of the referees would tell me that they're going to tell some schools about me. They would tell me that somebody needs me to play for them.

"There are a number of things that allowed me to achieve more than others who might have more physical ability than me. I think one of those things is having a vision. I think there's a difference between a vision and a dream. You know, a lot of people dream. Dreams are things that come and go. Dreams are things that you wish. I had a vision of myself being the best person I could be. I was reading books on having big dreams and the right attitude. I read many of Norman Vincent Peale's books. At thirteen, I would read anything by him that I could get my hands on. I started looking at the ads in the newspapers to find out where there were things going on to help make you a better person. Things like classes on how to buy real estate, save money, make money or negotiate—all kinds of things like that. I'd get on a bus and go twenty miles or more to go to one of these classes.

"At some point, like a light just came on, I began to realize that I was going somewhere. It was like the whole 'suitcase' thing from high school was coming alive, and I was destined to become somebody, destined to make a difference, destined to make a contribution wherever I was. I began to think that, whatever I was going to do with my life, I was going to make it better than it was before. I began to do these things in terms of exploring my world. I began to develop study groups to come to my home. We would have five, six, seven, or more guys come to my house to study together. That was in high school.

"I remember in the ninth grade I would often get up in the middle of the night and just go outside and take off running. Man, I'd just run and run and run. I'd run forwards. I'd run backwards. I'd run sideways. I'd see myself making great plays and great hits, and I'd see all the people screaming. I did this often. I'd also go sit up on this hill by my house and just look up to the sky, and I'd say, Lord, one day I'm going to make it. I'm just asking that You give me the courage to do what I need to do to be faithful to the calling that You've called me to.

"The bottom line is that there's a difference in a vision and a dream. A dream goes so far, and you have what I call a silent contract where internally you say I'm willing to go so far. If it gets too bad or hard, I can quit. A vision is when you say there's no turning back. You have no choice. You will succeed or die trying. That's what I was. It's what I was, and it's where I've been my entire life.

"If you have a strong vision of where you want to go, you have to focus on that vision. A lot of people talk about the focus I have. I think that was something that I was born with. I think there are many people born with that ability to focus. And that ability can either be cultivated or it can be crushed. If you put yourself around a group of people who cannot help to enhance your focus, then you're not going to develop as much of that as you could have. I believe that everything can be used for good or evil. Everything. It just depends on who and what we're around to influence us. The decisions we make and the choices that we make define what we're going to ultimately be.

"I wouldn't say that I had all my value systems in place by the time I was a teenager. I had certain inherent values—I was going to try my best, I wouldn't lie, and I'd try to help anybody I could. Even today, if I can help somebody, I'm going to do it. It's an honor for me to help someone—with no boundaries. If I'm on my way to a meeting and I see someone broke down on the side of the road, nine times out of ten, I'm going to stop and help. I might be late for the meeting, but I'm willing to suffer the consequences, because I remember what it was like as a kid when you were down and out with no one there to care. So, just to let somebody know that they're valuable enough for someone to stop and help is important to me. Whatever the situation, I'm going to be there for you. Those were the kinds of things I grew up with. And growing up in a church certainly reinforced those values.

"My mother played a huge part in my value system, too. We would talk for hours and hours at a time, sometimes from the time I got home from school till the next morning when the sun came up. We would talk about life. She would read me the bible, and we would pray. She would tell me about the mistakes she had made in her life and the mistakes my dad had made. We would talk about the kinds of things I needed to look out for if I was going to be successful. All those moments were a huge part in the development of my value systems.

"It's not an easy job to teach kids, and as far as any advice I might have for parents, let me tell you a story about one of my sons. Several years ago my son made the decision that he was no longer going to play baseball. Up until then, he was a darn good ball player. When the coaches pitched to him, he would knock the ball around pretty good. But when the kids his age started pitching to him, they didn't have that great of control and started popping him with the ball now and then. He was scared to death of the ball, but he didn't want me to know about it.

"When my wife told me that my son no longer wanted to play baseball I said, That's crazy, he loves baseball. So, I took him in my office and asked him why he didn't want to play anymore. He said, *Sir, I just don't like it anymore. It's not fun anymore.* I said, Son, you're exactly right. If it's not fun, there's no reason for you to play. Then I asked him to tell me that he absolutely did not want to play anymore...that he didn't enjoy his teammates and he didn't enjoy the game anymore, or if he was just afraid of the ball. I told him to look me in the eyes and be honest with me. I told him that he was a pretty good ball player and I hated to see him give it up if it was just because he was afraid of the ball, because if he was afraid of the ball we can work through that. But if you just don't want to play, I can't help you with that.

"My son just looked at me with a tear in his eye and said, *Dad, I'm afraid of the ball.* I said, That's great! Now let's create a plan and figure out what we're going to do. I can remember a coach telling me that it's very rare that a kid can overcome the fear of getting hit by the ball. So, we took our solution in phases. We started throwing tennis balls, got him back up next to the plate, and with the help of several other coaches, got him to overcome his fear of being hit. And now, he's back up to the plate making hits and home runs.

"When my son finally overcame his fear of the ball, I told him that, when I played football, I had something in my locker that said, *Success is not determined by what you achieve but by what you overcome.* I told him that I wanted him to understand that what he had done had nothing to do with hitting home runs. I wanted him to understand that what he had done was to overcome something, and that most people don't ever overcome things in their lives. To see him getting up to the plate just swinging, even if he struck out, is what life is all about. Swinging. Just give yourself a chance. It's 50-50 every time you swing. I told him that whatever he did, just keep swinging in life. That's the most important of things. And don't ever forget to thank God when you play and do wonderful things, because He gave you the courage to overcome the obstacles in your life.

"I think it's wrong for parents to take a game and make it some kind of performance deal for their kids. In other words, don't take your kids to McDonald's® for winning and take them home if they don't win. Don't critique every little thing they do on the field or on the court. Let the kids have fun.

"I'll have coaches sometimes call me and ask me what I think about a certain player. It'll be things like, *This kid doesn't know how to tackle, doesn't know how to block*...I'll ask, How old is the kid? *Ten years old.* Whoa, wait a minute! Let the kid have fun. This is the only chance he's got at this game, and if you dog the kid too hard you'll take away his chance to be what he might be.

"In my mind, before kids are around twelve years old, all sports are basically sandlot sports. There shouldn't be a commitment so big that the kids have to miss important family events. There is certainly a commitment level you want your kids to understand, but at these young ages, I think that the family commitment outweighs the athletic commitment. I think parents need to understand that family comes first, and if they can keep their focus on that and not let the performance of their kids affect who they are as parents, they'll be much better off, and the kids will, too."

* * *

It has been said that thoughts become the words that one will speak. The words that one speaks will become the actions that one takes. The actions that one takes will become habits. Those habits will ultimately become the character of the individual, and that character, revealed, is the destiny of a man or woman.

Destiny begins, always, with a choice. Ayn Rand, in her book *Atlas Shrugged,* relates, "Every man builds his world in his own image. He has the power to choose, but no power to escape the necessity of choice. If he abdicates his power, he abdicates the status of man, and the grinding chaos of the irrational is what he achieves as his sphere of existence—by his own choice."

The extent of a person's character ultimately becomes the measure of the choices a person makes. It's a non-negotiable fact of life. We occupy our minds with various thoughts and ultimately make choices in regard to those thoughts. Good and constructive thoughts typically lead to positive actions. Inversely, destructive patterns typically yield less favorable outcomes.

Life isn't something that just happens. It's sculpted from experience, exposure, perception, and our subsequent choices. Mike Singletary embraced his power to choose from an early age and created his life through the images of his thought—a life full of accomplishment as an athlete, and as a human being determined to live with honor.

Chapter 19

BART STARR

*Nothing can stop the man with the right mental attitude
from achieving his goal; nothing on earth can help the
man with the wrong mental attitude.*
— **W.W. Ziege**

B
ryan Bartlett Starr was born in Montgomery, Alabama, on January 9, 1934. He was the son of an Air Force NCO, and he played high school football at Lanier High School in Montgomery, Alabama, where he earned a spot in the school's Hall of Fame. Starr played college football at the University of Alabama and was a seventeenth round pick (200th overall) in the 1956 NFL draft.

Wearing number fifteen, Bart was quarterback for the Green Bay Packers from 1956-1971. Starr was a backup quarterback until 1959 when Vince Lombardi became coach of the Packers. Lombardi liked Bart's mechanics and, most of all, his decision-making abilities on the field. Under Lombardi's nurturing, Starr became one of the greatest field leaders in NFL history.

During his career, Starr's Packers won six divisional and five NFL championships ('61, '62, '65, '66, and '67)—the only player in history to quarterback a team to five NFL championships. Following the NFL championships, Bart led the Packers to championships in Super Bowls I and II where he was selected as the MVP in both of those games. Starr was selected to the Pro Bowl four times and was the NFL's Most Valuable Player in 1966. His jersey, number (15), is one of five numbers retired by the Green Bay Packers. While Starr never threw more than 300 passes per season, he still held several passing records, including the lifetime record of 57.4 percent completions over a sixteen-year period. Bart Starr was enshrined in the Pro Football Hall of Fame in 1977.

Immediately following his retirement as a player, Starr served as an assistant coach for Green Bay, later becoming the head coach in 1975 for nine seasons. In 1965, Bart and his wife, Cherry, helped co-found the Rawhide Boys Ranch in New London, Wisconsin, a facility for at-risk and troubled boys, and he remains affiliated with the ranch today. In 1999 he was ranked number 41 on *The Sporting News'* list of the 100 Greatest Football Players. Starr has an NFL award named after him, The Bart Starr Award, given by a panel of judges to the best Christian player in the NFL. Starr resides in Birmingham, Alabama, with his wife and is the chairman of Healthcare Realty Services.

66 **I**was born in Montgomery, Alabama, and I had one younger brother. My dad was in the military, and my mom was a homemaker. My dad worked for the state in the National Guard until WWII came along. He then became active in the U.S. Army. After the war, my dad transferred to the U.S. Air Force when the Army and Air Force separated. For most of my life, I grew up in a military family.

"My younger brother and I had a fun relationship. He was two years younger than I. We played lots of games in the neighborhood—things like hide-and-seek, tag, and other kinds of run-around and pickup games. We played a lot of pickup-type games in the sandlots and fields around the house. I can well remember taking lawn mowers—the push mowers without engines—and actually cutting out an infield and base paths where we could play pickup baseball games. It was competitive, but as an older brother, I also tried to be like a mentor to my brother.

"Our neighborhood was wonderful. Doors weren't locked at night. Everyone knew everybody else. There were plenty of kids around, and it was just a marvelous place to grow up in. As I got older, because my dad was in the military, we did live on some airbases as well. We moved around quite a bit. But, as I look back on my earlier life, the moving was a huge bonus to me because I was exposed to integration throughout my early life. Even though I basically grew up in the South, I didn't really know what segregation was, because I was playing all kinds of sports with black children.

"I was an avid sports fan as a kid, and my hero was Joe DiMaggio. I grew up idolizing him, and some others. I read about a lot of athletes like Don Hudson of the Green Bay Packers. Those were the types of individuals that you wanted to hopefully have a chance to be like one day when you grew up.

"My folks were very supportive of my athletic career. They were never pushy, but they were very, very supportive. My dad never really ever pushed me, but the big thing is that he helped me by going out in the back yard and playing with me. He would toss balls to us when we were learning how to catch and bat, and he would throw passes with us as we grew older. My folks attended a lot of my athletic events. They were avid fans and very supportive, yet they never interfered in a negative way. My dad was an extremely competitive person, and perhaps he was vicariously living out some of the things he would like to have been able to do through me. But both my parents were very supportive.

"My dad gave me some advice one day that really sticks with me. I wasn't very old, and the advice isn't necessarily just for athletics, but applies to life in general. He told me to please remember that you must earn someone's trust and respect. You can't expect them to give it to you. He also said don't ever give them yours—make them earn your respect as well. Later, as I got into athletics and began to play organized sports, he stressed to me the need to do the very best that you could do and give the greatest effort you can. Those were great pieces of advice.

"As far as playing sports, it was always my decision as to what I wanted to play or if I wanted to play. The only person who ever gave me a hard time about that was one of my uncles. He was a competitive athlete when he was younger, and he was always pushing me to play baseball. I was a big baseball fan, but when I went to college on a football scholarship, he really gave me a hard time. He told me that I just blew my career. He said I should have stayed with baseball. I've always laughed about that, even though he meant it in a lighthearted way.

"When it comes to role models, I would say that my parents were at the top of the list for the morals and ethics I have. I don't think that you can start at a better place than there. Of course, there were many others who had an influence on me.

"My high school coach played an inspirational role because he was a great leader. He was a superb, quality individual, and I told him numerous times over the years what an impact he had on me. In fact, I asked him to introduce me at my induction into the Pro Football Hall of Fame. Originally, I had asked my father to do it, but he told me no. My father told me he was honored that I asked him, but that I should have my high school coach do the introduction. So, I asked my high school coach, Bill Moseley, to introduce me.

"Coach Moseley helped me appreciate the need to be uniquely prepared and well organized. Of course, I saw this a lot in my father, too, because of his military background. One can have the greatest goals or the greatest plans, but it really comes down to executing those plans. If you don't execute the plan effectively, the plan isn't worth all that much. A good plan begins with preparation and organization.

"If you look at it in terms of trying to be the best you can be, the word **attitude** is a critical component to success. I came to appreciate the importance of attitude from my mother and father. They both had great attitudes. As I've matured through the years, I think everything I've accomplished is accountable, ultimately, to the word attitude. Even the preparation and organization that I talk about are just extensions of that word, attitude. I think that attitude is the strongest and most powerful word in our vocabulary, other than love. I think that every single thing that we do is a reflection of our attitude. I came to appreciate that from my high school coach.

"I'd like to think that the traits I have started with my family environment. But I also think that you further develop those traits as you move forward, mature, and experience life. When you start to describe the benefits of participation in sports, there are many words you can use to describe those benefits. Words like teamwork, discipline, sacrifice, competition, etc. But, when you really think about all those other words and qualities, they're all just extensions of the word attitude. For example, in order to make discipline a positive quality in your life, you've got to have the right attitude about it. Without the right attitude, the other qualities never have a chance to blossom and take hold.

"We've all got significant events and moments that happen in our lives. My brother passed away when he was ten years old, and I started to see my father in a different light after that. Looking back, my dad thought that my brother probably had a better chance at succeeding in athletics than I did. My father perceived him to be more competitive and tougher than I was, simply because my personality was more like my mother's. I was more introverted and had a little softer approach than my brother. My brother was more outgoing, and my father didn't really know what kind of fire I had within me, because I simply didn't show it.

"My father was a compassionate man, and when my brother passed away, I think he saw the need to work with me in a little different way. I can remember my dad mentioning to me that he wasn't sure that I was going to be strong or tough enough mentally to do certain things. All that did was just challenge me more. It was like, I'll show you!

"I was blessed with growing up in a unique atmosphere. My father was a driven person, and because of the military side of him, I think that added a dimension that enabled me to be more like that. Without pushing, shoving, or erratically doing something, it was more like this was the structure, this was the organization, the discipline and commitment that you saw every day of your life that you lived with this man. He did that in a loving way, and that was just the structure of our household. And I don't want to forget my mother, because she was the bedrock of the family, especially when my father was oversees or on some kind of assignment. She was a great lady.

"I think the most important word to describe any success I might have had would be the word **team**. Team starts with family. Team is a place in church or in the workplace. Just about everything you do is done from the team viewpoint. I was privileged to be a part of a great team structure everywhere I was. In high school, we had excellent players who were great individuals and solid players. In college, we had the same thing. And I could not have been more blessed than to have been in such a great environment with so many great teammates in Green Bay. I had some mental toughness and courage, but I didn't have the physical talent of a lot of people. But I was blessed by being with a very strong team.

"Of course, there's another individual that had a tremendous impact on me as a player and as a person. Coach Lombardi. I remember when he came to the Packers. He opened his first session by thanking the Green Bay organization for giving him this opportunity, then quickly turned to us players and said, *Gentlemen, we're going to relentlessly chase perfection, knowing full well we will not catch it, because perfection is not attainable. We're going to relentlessly chase it because, in the process, we will catch excellence.* Then he paused for a moment and said, *I am not remotely interested in being just good.* Now that's how he opened the first session we had with him. That's how he opened it, and how he lived it until the day he left Green Bay. I remember it had such an impact on me that when we got our first break, I ran downstairs and called my wife and I said, Honey, we're going to begin to win! He had an impact on us every day for nine years. It was a great experience.

"As far as any advice I might have for parents today, one thing that parents need to understand is that the most noble form of leadership is through example. Kids will soak up what they see, so as parents, you've got to try and optimize good exposure for your kids.

"General Douglas MacArthur had a great quote that relates to the importance of athletic endeavor. I've always been awed by this quote. The story goes that a young writer had asked for permission to interview the General, which the General granted. The young writer asked General MacArthur if he was a staunch advocate of athletics when he was commandant at West Point years earlier. General MacArthur replied, *Young man, the infinite values of athletic competition have intensified with the passage of time. It is a vital character builder, as it molds a youth of our country for their future roles as custodians of the Republic. Fathers and mothers who would have their sons and daughters become men and women should have them play the game. For, on the field of friendly strife, are sewn the seeds which on other fields and future years will bear the fruits of victory. That says it all, don't you think?"*

* * *

When we're born, we begin our life experience at a value of about zero. Aside from the innate things we know as an infant, such as hunger and pain, we're essentially a blank slate—ready to be embossed and defined by the inevitable experiences of life.

What then are the critical characteristics that enable us to be successful in life? Is it knowledge? Hard work? Attitude? If you assign a numerical value to each of the letters in these words, and add those letters up, you've got your answer. (For example: a=1, b=2, c=3, d=4, etc.)

K=11, **N**=14, **O**=15, **W**=23, **L**=12, **E**=5, **D**=4, **G**=7, **E**=5	96
H=8, **A**=1, **R**=18, **D**=4, **W**=23, **O**=15, **R**=18, **K**=11	98
A=1, **T**=20, **T**=20, **I**=9, **T**=20, **U**=21, **D**=4, **E**=5	100

The disposition of your mind, your attitude, is the springboard for all that follows. Greatness is largely a by-product of attitude, and those who achieve greatness in any endeavor have at their core a simple and powerful attribute, which dictates the terms by which an individual will pursue his/her mission. Whatever is required—hard work, discipline, courage, teamwork or any other quality—an *attitude* accompanies that quality and either makes it a winning quality or a defeating quality.

Bart Starr learned how to harness the positive power of *attitude* to become one of the greatest quarterbacks ever to play the game of football. He understood that he had a choice to develop and manifest that attitude. He understood that to do less, on or off the field, was an unacceptable alternative.

Chapter 20

JOHNNY UNITAS

*What this power is, I cannot say. All I know is that it
exists...and it becomes available only when you are in that
state of mind in which you know exactly what you want...
and are fully determined not to quit until you get it.*

— Alexander Graham Bell

John Constantine "Johnny" Unitas (May 7, 1933-September 11, 2002) was born in Pittsburgh, Pennsylvania. He was raised by his Lithuanian mother, who worked two jobs to support the family after the death of his father when Unitas was five years old. He played high school football at St. Justin's High School in Pittsburgh, playing halfback and quarterback.

Unitas played college football at the University of Louisville where he played quarterback. At Louisville, he completed 245 passes for 3,139 yards and twenty-seven touchdowns. In the 1952 season at Louisville, the university president reduced the amount of athletic aid, which resulted in the team having to play one-platoon football. Unitas played safety or linebacker on defense, quarterback on offense and returned kicks on special teams.

In a game against Tennessee in 1953, Unitas completed nine of nineteen passes, rushed nine times, returned six kickoffs, one punt, and had eighty-six percent of the team's tackles. The only touchdown the Louisville Cardinals scored was when Unitas faked a pitch and ran the ball twenty-three yards for a TD. He was hurt late in the fourth quarter, and on the way off the field, he received a standing ovation. When he got to the locker room, he had to have his jersey and shoulder pads cut off because he was so fatigued he couldn't lift his arms.

Unitas was drafted by the Pittsburgh Steelers in 1955 in the ninth round. He was cut by the Steelers before the season began. At that time, he was married and had a child and worked construction to support his family. On weekends, he played for a local semi-pro team, the Bloomfield Rams, for $6 a game.

In 1956, Unitas joined the Baltimore Colts under legendary Coach Weeb Eubank after being asked by a Bloomfield teammate to join him for a tryout in Baltimore. The Colts signed Unitas, much to the chagrin of the Cleveland Browns, who had hoped to sign him.

In the first overtime game in NFL history, also dubbed as "the greatest game ever played," the Colts and Unitas won the NFL Championship in 1958, defeating the New York Giants. The Colts repeated their championship efforts the next season, again against the Giants. Unitas was named the NFL MVP in 1959 by UPI and AP.

Unitas holds the record for most consecutive touchdown passes at forty-seven games, which ended in the 1960 season. He also led the league in total passing yards (3,481) and completions (237) that year.

In 1964, Unitas was named for a second time as the NFL MVP by UPI and AP. In 1967, Unitas received his third NFL MVP award.

In 1973, Unitas was traded to the San Diego Chargers, and he retired from professional football after seventeen NFL seasons.

Unitas was the first quarterback to throw for more than 40,000 yards. He holds the record for most Pro Bowl appearances by a quarterback (ten). He was MVP of three Pro Bowls. He was selected nine times as an All-Pro. He won three NFL Championships and one Super Bowl (V). He was awarded the Bert Bell Award three times and received the Walter Payton Man of the Year award in 1970. In 1999, Unitas was named number five on *The Sporting News'* list of the 100 Greatest Football Players. He was voted into the Pro Football Hall of Fame in 1979.

He died of a heart attack on September 11, 2002, while working out at a physical therapy facility in Lutherville-Timonium, Maryland, at age sixty-nine. He's considered by many to be the best quarterback to ever play professional football.

" I was born in Pittsburgh on May 7, 1933, in a little suburb called Brookline. I had one older brother and two sisters, one older, one younger. My mother was a housewife, and my father had a coal truck that he used to deliver coal to people's homes. He would go up to the mines and get coal in the morning, then deliver the coal to different homes all day long.

"When I was five years old, my father died of pneumonia, and we moved over to an area called Mt. Washington because we couldn't afford to stay where we were. Mt. Washington looked right over the edge of downtown Pittsburgh. It was a mixed neighborhood with blacks, Italians, and Polish families. It was a nice area to live because you had plenty of kids, and you always played in the streets. Everybody seemed to be happy, and nobody ever had any problems as far as crime. Of course, there were a couple of bad eggs there, but it was a good variety of people.

"We always were playing something when I was a kid—basketball, football, softball, or anything like that. I was never in organized sports until high school. I don't recall any particular influence to play sports. It was all you had to do. You played whatever was in season. Nobody really influenced me to play. I didn't have any athletic role models.

"My mother was always concerned that I was going to get hurt, so she never played a big role in my career, whatsoever. As far as what kind of person I am, I did learn more from my mother than I did from anybody else. She was head of the household, and she set the law down, and you didn't vary from what she said too often. You had certain chores to do, you had to be home at a certain time—those are the kinds of things that you were expected to do.

"My high school football coach, Jim Max Carey, played a big part in my development, both as an individual and as a football player. He took a particular liking to me, and he would take me to basketball games. He took me to my first professional football game ever in Cleveland in 1950. That's the only professional football game I had ever seen in my life. He was very instrumental in keeping my interest and talking to me about keeping on the right side of the law and everything else. It was easy to get in trouble where I came from because there were always a bunch of guys hanging around on a street corner, you know, doing this and doing that. He always had one particular saying, *When the going gets tough, the tough get going. Anybody can do it when it's easy.* That had a big impact on me.

"There wasn't any magic moment or particular event that made me what I am. I just went out and played and did what I knew how to do. I did what the coaches asked me to do and played within the framework of a team effort, more so than from an individual standpoint. If you had the talent, then you played every sport there was. I was at the playground all the time. We played basketball, horseshoes, softball, tennis, swimming—whatever they had in the playground, you name it, we played it.

"We sort of looked at my older brother as the head of the family when he turned sixteen. He more or less took on that aspect because he got his license, and he drove a truck and delivered coal in the morning before school. He was sort of the father figure of the household until he went into the service. Then it was just my mom, and she went to work every day at seven o'clock in the morning. She had a couple of different jobs. She ended up being a bookkeeper for the city, and in between, she worked in the bakery and cleaned offices at night.

"We learned early on that everybody had to pitch in for the household. My sisters did the washing, ironing, and cooking. Breakfast would be on the table when my mom left for work. It was usually some kind of oatmeal. You didn't get the bacon and eggs from the pan right to your plate, I can tell you that!

"My success is as simple as having the desire to be successful, the desire to want to exceed in whatever you want to do. I had fun with it. It wasn't hard work for me; it was just something I did all of my lifetime. I played every sport in high school, but we only had basketball and football. But down on the playground, you played all kinds of stuff.

"What people look at as hard work, as far as practice, that was fun for me. And who really knows what kind of natural talent you're born with. You play and you're interested in something, and you work at it. It wasn't all fun and games. I worked a lot of hard hours by myself throwing balls against tires, fences, and things like that. You didn't always have other people out there to help you. You did what you wanted to do. It wasn't a big deal. You just did it.

"I think you have your basic fundamental values in place by the time you're around eight years old, and as you're growing up, you add to those. The basic fundamentals of living are set by your parents—what they do for you, the rules and regulations they set, and how you abide by them.

"I don't see what's so difficult for people nowadays because life is very simple. You get up, you go to work, you do what you're supposed to do, and that's it. People get microscopic about things these days. It would be better if people had common sense, rather than book sense, and used it. I've known lawyers and professionals who graduated magna cum laud who don't have enough sense to get out of the rain. This country is lacking good common sense in a lot of different areas and in a lot of people.

"My advice for parents today would be to set the rules and regulations of what you want your children to abide by and stay with those rules, and don't give an inch away. You set a rule, enforce discipline when the rule is broken, and throw the psychology book in the trash. All the bull about psychology, worry about this and worry about how the kid's going feel, to me is ridiculous.

"There are rules, and there are regulations. It's like I told my kids, we have rules and if you step over the rules, then you're going to pay the fiddler. If you want to break the rules that bad, you pay the fiddler—you're going to get your privilege taken away. If that's what you want, I can do that. It's not a problem for me to do that. And I've never had a problem. I've got eight children, and I've never had a problem out of any of them.

"Take interest in what the kids are doing. Try to go to every one of their ball games, or whatever, and just be interested in their life. Try to involve yourself in what they're interested in. But never get away from the discipline factor.

"Parents today are afraid of their children. They're afraid to discipline them because they might tell a teacher or counselor at school. If one of my kids did that, they would have gotten their butts whipped twice as bad when they got home. But I never had to whip my kids very often. They got a strap across their backside once or twice, and that's all they needed. I believe kids are asking for discipline. They do things to be disciplined for. If the parents don't provide the discipline, you're going to have a problem."

* * *

It's been said that tragedies are like knives. Depending upon how you hold the knife, by the handle or by the blade, tragedy can either serve you or cut you. So it is with life, too. When external events tend to cause distress to a person, it's not really the event that causes pain—it's your own estimation of it. And one has the conscious power to retract this estimation or empower it.

A young Johnny Unitas suffered a tragedy the day his father died, and I'm sure it wouldn't have been a surprise to anyone if Johnny wouldn't have amounted to much in his life. As history has revealed, however, it's pretty apparent that he took the knife by the handle and carved out a pretty impressive life and career, in fact, a life many consider to be as the best quarterback to ever play professional football, bar none.

John Unitas wasn't a complicated man. No pomp and circumstance. No punk ego. No visions of grandeur. He was a simple man with an extraordinary ability to focus on his mission and provide the leadership and courage to meld a group of men together who played some of the best football ever played by a team.

Chapter 21

KELLEN WINSLOW

*The dreams I only thought about, the ones I took
no action on, well they are still dreams. But the
ones that I took action on, they are now a reality.*
— Catherine Pulsifer

Kellen Boswell Winslow was born on November 5, 1957, in St. Louis, Missouri. He's the third oldest of seven children. He is widely recognized as one of the greatest tight ends to ever play professional football—a significant fact, since his first exposure to organized football didn't occur until his senior year in high school.

Winslow played college football at the University of Missouri and was drafted in the first round of the 1979 NFL Draft by the San Diego Chargers and played for them until 1987 when injuries forced his retirement.

Along with Ozzie Newsome, Mike Ditka, John Mackey, and Dave Casper, Winslow is frequently credited with redefining the position of tight end from a position of primarily blocker and short route receiver, to a downfield receiver with great athletic ability and speed.

Kellen led the NFL in receptions in 1980 and 1981, becoming the first tight end to ever lead the league in back-to-back seasons. He exceeded 1,000 yards receiving in three different seasons and still holds the single season record for receiving yards by a tight end with 1,290 yards in the 1980 season.

In a 1981 season playoff game with Miami, known as the "Epic in Miami," Winslow caught thirteen passes for 166 yards and blocked a field goal attempt with seconds remaining to send the game into overtime. During that game he was treated for a pinched nerve in his shoulder, dehydration, severe cramps, and received three stitches in his lip. The image of his teammates helping him off the field after the game is one of the most enduring images in NFL lore.

Kellen played in five Pro Bowls, was a four time All-Pro selection, was named to the NFL 75th Anniversary All-Time Team, and the NFL 1980s All-Decade Team, was the 1982 co-Pro Bowl MVP, was ranked number 73 on the 1999 *The Sporting News'* list of the 100 Greatest Football Players, elected to the San Diego Chargers Hall of Fame, the College Hall of Fame in 2002, and the Pro Football Hall of Fame in 1995.

Kellen worked as a college football announcer with Fox Sports Net after his retirement and is currently the Athletic Director of Central State University in Ohio. Winslow's son also plays professional football as a tight end and was drafted in the first round of the 2004 NFL Draft.

66 I was born in St. Louis, Missouri, but I was raised in East St. Louis, Illinois, across the river from St. Louis. The reason I was born in St. Louis was because African Americans couldn't go to the hospital in East St. Louis in 1957. I'm the third oldest of seven children, four girls and three boys. I'm the oldest boy of the family.

"My father worked as a bus driver for Bi-State Transit. He was one of the first African Americans to be hired by Bi-State Transit. My mother worked at various occupations, but I remember her working most of the time at Sears and Roebuck. She worked in the accounting department and the sales department.

"We grew up in a middle-to-lower middle class kind of neighborhood. We never wanted for anything. We had plenty to eat and always had clothes to wear. With both parents working, we did okay. In fact, we did very well.

"Both of my parents stayed married as I grew up, and they're still married today. When I was very young, we moved from the projects called Cleveland Avenue to the house I grew up in. But I grew up in the same city until I went off to college.

"The first organized sport I played was baseball when I was a sophomore in high school. A little earlier than that I played some baseball in what they called the Quarry League. Everything else we did, sports-wise, was just a sandlot organization kind of thing. We had enough kids in the neighborhood to play different kinds of sandlot games.

"When I was a sophomore and junior in high school, I worked for UPS. I didn't play any organized football until my senior year in high school. And that was only because my gym teacher, who was also the football coach, encouraged me to come out for the football team because I had some size and speed. But one of my biggest incentives to play was the potential for a college scholarship. That was a big lure for me.

"My parents didn't have much of a role in my playing sports. With seven kids to raise and both parents working, the older kids did most of the day-to-day rearing. But my parents had a strong presence in the home. We had a strong and close family nuclear unit. I had cousins, aunts, uncles, and grandparents who lived just down the street from us. While we were a close family, my parents had little to do with my athletic involvement.

"It was rare if my parents ever got the chance to come to a baseball game. But that wasn't a big deal because I understood that they had to work and didn't have the time to attend my games. I'm certainly not going to go to therapy because my parents didn't come to all my games and think that they didn't love me. It was quite the opposite. I knew they loved me because they went to work for me and put a roof over my head, food in my mouth, and clothes on my back. Occasionally, they would even put a little change in my pocket.

"Playing sports wasn't always my decision, though. I remember I wanted to play football in the seventh grade. The coach wanted me to come out for the junior high team. My dad knew the coach, and it was okay with him, but my mother said no, and she won that battle. I joke about it now and say I could have been somebody if she would have let me go out for football in the seventh grade. But she was afraid I might get hurt, so she wouldn't let me play.

"She did finally relent when I was in the tenth grade and let me go out for football. I went out for two days and decided that football wasn't for me, and didn't come back until my senior year. That wasn't a problem at all with my parents, but I think it's probably a dangerous lesson to learn, to allow your kids not to follow through with their commitment.

"Kids should do something athletically, and they should have opportunities to experiment with different sports. But if they start, they need to finish the season out. If you let them quit, that's detrimental in the long run. Learning to quit is a dangerous lesson to learn, because you'll start to do that in other phases of your life. It's so easy to walk away when things get a little tough.

"As far as athletic role models are concerned, high school sports were huge in East St. Louis, Illinois. It was almost as if you were a legend if you played high school football in East St. Louis. The people who played on the teams before you had a big image in the community, and you often heard people talking about the basketball and football players around town. So, there was quite a large degree of recognition as a high school athlete around my town.

"On a professional level, the Green Bay Packers was my favorite team. I don't know exactly why Green Bay was my favorite team. I didn't even know where Green Bay was when I was in high school. I guess you just saw them more on television at that time, and they had a great program with great players and coaches and always seemed to be at the top of the heap.

"Morally and spiritually, all my significant role models were right there in our home, and it included my entire extended family—uncles, aunts, and grandparents—along with my parents. Church was an important component in our family, and on Sunday, that's where we would be. Sometimes they might have to drag us kids to church, but on Sunday you went to church. And we participated in church activities, such as the Easter play, the Christmas pageant, and singing in the choir. My family and the environment that my family operated in provided a solid moral base for me.

"Even though I didn't play football until my senior year in high school, that experience had a tremendous impact on me, too. My high school coaches were like master psychologists and teachers. I wasn't aware of it at the time, but as I look back at that experience, you become more aware of what the coaches were trying to do with you.

"One of the things I remember most is that our coaches were never trying to pull you down or denigrate you. It seems like everything they did was designed to build you up in some way, and to present you with challenges to help you grow to be a better athlete and a better person. I can't thank them enough for the things they did for me. I was just a young, naïve, and insecure kid, and after a short year of playing football and being exposed to their wonderful leadership, I guess you might say I came out of my shell and became a better person for that experience.

"I owe an awful lot to those coaches. After all, they're the ones who got me to come out for football, and I guess they used a little psychology on me to get me to play. They spent some time trying to get me to play, but they never did pressure me in any way.

"I remember I'd be coming out of a class and Coach Perry would be standing outside of the classroom waiting on me. He would say, *Son*, (it was always son), *come here. I don't think you realize what you have and what you're capable of doing.* I remember thinking, What are you talking about? He would talk about the way I could run and catch the ball, and he'd talk about how I was able to kind of take charge of my gym class. He would put an image in my mind by saying something like, *I hope you realize what you've got and what it means,* then always encourage me to think about coming out for football. Then he would just walk away and leave me there, thinking about what he said.

"Then a few days later, he would show up and go through the same kind of exercise with me. All of this was around the end of my junior year in high school. He worked on me all summer long. Finally, I took a leave of absence from my UPS job and came out for football. It always impressed me that he never pressured me or tried to embarrass me to come out for the team. He always dealt with me as a human being with great respect.

"Coach Perry wasn't the only one working on me, either. The assistant coach, Coach Lewis, was involved, too. Sometimes it seemed like they were a tag team. They had played running backs together at our high school. They went off to college together, and they came back and coached together. Then they both left coaching and went into counseling, then into administration. It's like they were an inseparable team. It's incredible the things they did for the young people at our school.

"They even got the principal of the school to work on me. Come to find out, the principal had taken my mom to the high school prom years ago and kind of knew the whole family. So, when he realizes I'm part of that family, he catches me in the hall and pulls me into his office and asked me what I was going to do. Kind of sarcastically, he said, *You don't have to play football now. You can always do it when you're twenty-four years old.* Then he would put it in perspective to help me realize that high school only comes around one time, and you don't get a second chance at a missed opportunity like this.

"I remember one time both coaches talking to me and asking me what I was going to do. I told them my plans were to work at my UPS job, go to a two-year college, then go to a four-year school to finish my degree. I remember them just kind of shaking their heads when I told them that. Then they asked me if I ever thought about going to a four-year school right away. I said that would be great, but how am I going to do that?

"That's when they hit me with the statement—and I'll never forget this—that they didn't see any reason whatsoever that after a year with them on the football team that I shouldn't be in some man's college on a football scholarship. Remember, they had been working on me for weeks, but with that statement they had me hook, line, and sinker. They were smart guys and one of the great blessings I've had in my life.

"They had me in their grip at that point, and I trusted them both. When I needed to be chastised for something, they chastised me. When I needed to be challenged, they challenged me. But it was never without some kind of encouragement. They were such an influence on me that I wanted both of them to be my presenters at my Pro Football Hall of Fame induction. But I could only choose one, so Coach Perry, being the head coach, was the logical choice.

"I didn't realize it at the time, but it was like a mini-conspiracy of people working on me, trying to get me to play football. As I look back on all of that, I realize it wasn't about trying to recruit a good prospect who might help the team. It was more about creating an opportunity for a kid who didn't have a clue about the advantages that participating in athletics could bring.

"These guys were just mental geniuses who had an incredible ability to provide positive direction for a kid like me. I think a lot of that kind of thing is lost today. There are so many coaches out there today, dealing with every age group, who don't teach and don't challenge in an encouraging way. They just yell and scream and only think about the X's and O's that are on the paper in a purely mechanistic way, often sacrificing the other positive dimensions that athletics can bring to a person.

"As far as my success in football, I think there are a combination of factors involved in that. The nurturing I got from my environment growing up helped develop who I was and how I saw things. Of course, I had some natural ability, but without the family environment, the coaches, and other influences, having talent doesn't guarantee that you'll be successful. So, all the various factors gave me an attitude that I wanted to be different and not just another face in the crowd.

"My parents always challenged me to do more and be more. I remember I worked at a place shining shoes when I was a kid, because I wanted to make some money. My father didn't tell me I couldn't do that, but he did let me know that he wanted something more than that for me. His expectation was like a challenge for me to take another step up the ladder, so I used that shoe shining moment to latch onto something else.

"I remember the summer after my freshman year at Missouri I went to work in a munitions plant. One day, after putting in a double shift, I remember just looking around at the other workers there. Some of them had been there for thirty or more years. I remember having the realization that I didn't want to spend the next thirty-five years doing this job. Don't get me wrong, these were fine, hard working people with good lives, but it just wasn't what I was looking for. When I went back to school, I started paying more attention, because I realized I was looking for more than that kind of employment offered. I challenged myself to be more.

"That day in the munitions factory is a day that I remember very clearly and is another example of challenging myself to take another step up the ladder. Another critical moment in my high school football career was in the first game I played in. I was about as green and naïve as you could be and just innocent about how a game should go. I wasn't even aware that the game had started, and I was in a daze about what was going on. Another player even had to tell me to get my helmet on because I was supposed to be in the game. I was a step behind for the entire game.

"I got a ball thrown in my direction, and I remember getting hit hard in the back, and I went back to the sidelines and sat on the bench, almost in tears. The coaches came over and asked if I was okay, and several of the players said something to me, but what I really remember is sitting on that bench and making a decision. I was either going to get up off the bench and finish the game or sit there and never play again.

"That was a difficult decision, because I'd never been hit like that before, and I didn't have any basis to compare or measure how bad I was actually hurt. But I got up off the bench, and with the encouragement of my teammates, got back into the game and eventually caught a pass. And when I caught that first pass, I realized that I could do this.

"Our next game had a play designed for me to block a linebacker to open up a hole for the fullback. I got a couple of good licks in on that particular play, and the coaches made a pretty big deal out of it after the game. When we watched the game film on the following Monday, the coaches made an announcement to the team and said they wanted everybody to pay attention to Winslow on the film.

"The film of the play starts and the fullback is moving to the hole, and you can see the linebacker looking at the fullback, ready to pounce on him. I come in from the right side and just level the linebacker. The entire room went into a roar: Winslow! Winslow! Winslow! I could have just floated right out of that room at that moment. That was my second football game, and it just made me hungrier and encouraged me that much more. That moment helped me realize that I could play at this level, and it gave me a huge surge of confidence. It was at that point that I really started to study the game more seriously.

"Professionally, the playoff game against Miami comes to mind. They call it the Epic In Miami. We were up twenty-four to seven, or twenty-four to nothing in the second quarter, and I remember our team already celebrating on the sideline. Charlie Joiner, the consummate professional, is sitting on the bench, and I go over to him and ask him what's wrong? He shakes his head and says that we're getting complacent, and we shouldn't be celebrating this early in the game. I can still remember what he said: *You don't do this to a Don Shula team in the playoffs. He's going to pull David Woodley and put Don Strock in and start throwing the football. We're going to be here all day.*

"And he was right. The very next series Shula put in Strock and started throwing the football. By half time it was twenty-four to twenty-one. I remember saying to Charlie Joiner that there was no way we were going to lose this ball game and that I refused to be a part of a team that ended up losing a game where we were up by twenty-four points. I got mad to the point that it added resolve to the commitment I had to win this ball game.

"When Miami came back out after half time, they took the lead, and it went back and forth till the end of the game. People have asked me many times how I managed to keep coming back out on the field, because I was pretty battered up and dehydrated. The fact is, I was going to do whatever it took to be a part of winning that game and, as long as I could get up and move, you were going to get every ounce of what I had to offer. And it didn't matter how many more quarters we would have to play in overtime. I would still have been out there. I remember that moment, and I remember that feeling.

"Those are some of the examples of how my values translated into performance on the field. I mentioned before I believe it was a combination of things that resulted in the compilation of your character and values. We grew up being taught to treat people with respect. I still don't address my coaches by their first names. I call them coach out of respect for their position.

"We learned these things when we were kids going to church. Our parents consistently instilled these values. I've never had any problem with the way my parents raised me. If they needed to beat my butt, that's what happened. They never abused me, they corrected me. And they showed me a lot of love and affection. They took care of me, they challenged me, and they punished me when I needed to be punished. They did a wonderful job, and I tell them that. They taught us good, positive values at an early age, and sports helped reinforce those values in my case.

"The combination of influences I had in my life shaped the way I looked at life and lived my life. On the football field I was a strong advocate of hard work, and it wasn't really about trying to meet someone else's expectations, it was more about trying to meet the expectations I placed on myself. One of the best compliments I ever received was from one of the trainers for the Chargers. He came up to me one day and told me that one of the things that people don't realize about me is how hard I work in practice. On game day it might look easy, but that was because we worked our tails off in practice.

"When we hit the practice field, we never stopped running, and you play the games the way that you practice. I remember I hated those two-a-day practices. But once you got started, you wanted to run as many plays and catch as many passes as you could. Unless you've been there, you just don't realize the level of work and effort that goes into practice.

"Even as hard as you work at being as good as you can be, you're still not ever completely satisfied with your performance—at least that's the way I felt. I caught thirteen passes for 166 yards in one game. What I think about is the two that I dropped, and I can tell you more about the pass that hit me right in the hands, that I dropped, than I can about the thirteen that I caught. I don't think any great players are ever completely satisfied with the way that they played. When you start thinking that way, it's time to do something else.

"For me, it wasn't about having some kind of obsession with perfection or meeting other peoples' expectations. It was more about self-challenge and meeting the expectations that I put on myself. I set my expectations high, and if I came close to meeting those, then everybody else's expectations were taken care of anyway.

"If you look back, you can always find plays where you wish you would have worked a little harder to get a better block, run a quicker pattern, or put forth just a little more effort. It's the self-challenge and the self-expectation that drives you to get the most out of your potential. I think you need that. That's what separates the good ones from the great ones. The great ones are never completely satisfied.

"As far as any advice I might have for parents and their kids, I would simply say, if you're going to participate in something, give it all you've got. I think you see a lot of people who have the talent and ability to be good at something, but they don't put forth the effort that's required.

"Take Michael Jordan, for example. What made him such a great basketball player? He worked hard at it and paid attention to detail. He didn't even make the high school basketball team as a sophomore. That just motivated him to work harder, and that commitment and work transformed him into the best basketball player to ever play the game. It didn't just happen. He worked his tail off.

"If you're going to be involved in something, you need to work at it, because if you don't, you get into bad habits that carry over into other areas of your life. My youngest son plays professional football now, but I always stressed the importance of work to him in his younger days.

"I remember he was attending a football camp in high school one summer, and I was watching him, and he was just dragging around. I told him that he wasn't working like he needed to be, and when he went back out on the field, he still wasn't working. People might think it's cruel, or whatever, but I got him, and we left. I told him if you're not going to work at it, you're just wasting your time and mine.

"You can have fun, but you have to work. In fact, I think the harder that you work, the more fun it is. It's definitely more fun to be on the winning side than it is to be on the losing side. It's a pretty good bet that the winning team put in more work than the losing team. You play the way you practice. That applies to athletics and life."

* * *

In 1687 Sir Isaac Newton published a book to help explain and investigate the motion of physical objects and systems. That work is framed around three basic laws of motion, and the first law is the Law of Inertia.

Basically, the Law of Inertia states that a body at rest remains at rest, and a body in motion stays in motion—unless it's acted upon by an external force.

While Newton was more interested in mathematical explanations for the motion of physical objects, it's interesting to see how his Law of Inertia applies to the expression of potential and success in our life.

Human beings are always making a choice to be at some degree of rest, or to be at some degree of motion, and the degree at which they operate has an enormous affect on how successful they are. For example, assume one has a pile of rocks he wants to move from point A to point B. The more successful conclusion to this task is to stay in motion, moving the rocks as effectively as you can. It's impossible to complete the task if you remain at rest. There must be action to accomplish the task.

When you're in a state of motion and taking action in any endeavor, a number of other things happen along the way. For example, an athlete who strives to do his best over a period of time dramatically improves his efficiencies and proficiencies. Because he's developed those skills so well, perhaps he gets the opportunity to receive an athletic scholarship to college. The point is that action breeds opportunity. The more action you invest in an activity, any activity, the more doors of opportunity will open for you—opportunities that you may have never even imagined.

Kellen Winslow always had a plan, but when he was a junior in high school, never having played organized football, he never imagined, in his wildest dreams, that his plan for a college education would be fulfilled through a football scholarship. He had talent, but he also had inertia, took action, and walked through the door when opportunity came knocking. That's just how life is. You make a choice, input action, take advantage of the opportunities you create, and live with the outcomes. The degree of your success is proportional to the degree of your inertia, and that's only limited by your degree of commitment.

Chapter 22

STEVE YOUNG

---

*The achievement of your goal is assured
the moment you commit yourself to it.*

— Mack R. Douglas

Steve Young was born in Salt Lake City, Utah, on October 11, 1961. He attended Greenwich High School in Greenwich, Connecticut, and earned All-FCIAC Team Honors his junior and senior years, 1978 and 1979. Additionally, he received CIAC All-State honors in 1979 and served as co-captain of the football, basketball, and baseball teams as a senior. Steve was a National Merit Scholar and posted a 4.0 GPA.

Steve played college football at Brigham Young University in Salt Lake City, Utah. While quarterback at BYU, the university set a NCAA record by averaging 584.2 yards of total offense per game, 370.5 of those yards coming from Young's passing and rushing. Young was named First Team All-American and finished second in voting for the Heisman Trophy.

In 1984, Young signed a record $40 million contract with the Los Angeles Express of the now defunct USFL. In 1985, Young signed with the Tampa Bay Buccaneers after being the first selection in that year's supplemental draft. After a less than stellar two-year stint with Tampa Bay, Young was traded to the San Francisco 49ers in 1987 to become a backup for Joe Montana. Young became the starting quarterback in his eighth season with the 49ers, and while he only played two full seasons during his fifteen-year career, he has the highest passer rating (96.8) of any quarterback in the NFL.

During his career he made 232 touchdowns and had 107 interceptions, while gaining a total of 33,124 yards. He holds the record for
the most rushing touchdowns by a quarterback (forty-three) and is
tied for the most passing titles (six). He attended the Pro Bowl seven
times, won three Super Bowl rings, and was voted MVP in Super Bowl
XXIX in 1995. He was voted MVP of the NFL in 1992 and 1994. He's
a member of the College Hall of Fame and was inducted into the Pro
Football Hall of Fame in 2005.

Young is the great-great-great grandson of Brigham Young, second
president of The Church of Jesus Christ of Latter-day Saints. He married former model Barbara Graham in 2000, and they are the parents
of three children, two sons and one daughter.

" **I** was born in Salt Lake City, Utah. I've got three younger
brothers and one younger sister. My dad is a lawyer, and
my mom is a housewife. My siblings were involved in sports,
and it was always very competitive around our house. We lived in a
neighborhood with a lot of kids till I was eight years old. Then we
moved from Utah to Connecticut, but that neighborhood had lots of
kids, too. The first organized sport I played was baseball at seven years
old. I started playing football when I was eight.

"Playing sports was kind of like drinking water. Everyone did it, so
I started playing. I kind of played every sport, and it was always my
choice. I had to go to all the practices and, as long as I did that, and
didn't quit, I could play whatever I wanted. The big rule my dad had
about sports was that I couldn't quit something once I started it. His
biggest concern was that I would be a quitter in life. I think he wanted
to make sure that I understood that, once you start the process of
quitting, you never got out of that mindset. It was like a rock rolling
downhill. He would say that once you start quitting you allow that
to infect your life. He was big on doing whatever you had agreed to
do. You just didn't quit. We would even skip summer vacations and
other things because my dad had made the point, if you committed

to something, you had to fulfill your commitment. I gained a real respect for practice because we sacrificed those other things for it.

"My greatest athletic role model was Roger Staubach, the great Dallas Cowboys quarterback. He was my hero, and I grew up watching him. My greatest moral role model was my dad. One of the earliest critical moments I can remember was when I was about thirteen years old. I was the youngest guy on the baseball team, and I really wanted to do well, but I didn't do very well. That was the first real failure in my life at that time. I had to deal with that and the way it made me feel, and I remember that was a real big issue to me. It was a moment of growth, you might say.

"My high school football coach had a lot of influence on me. He was always the guy you wanted to impress the most. I remember one time in the tenth grade, on the JV team, he came in to the locker room after a game and told us we were the worst group of athletes he had ever seen. You might say it was motivation through humiliation. That inspired us to try to do better. As a group we worked hard to become better after that. We never were state champions, but we won the county championship after that, and that was a real big deal for all of us.

"I've always been pretty relentless in my approach to everything. I never missed anything. I never missed a day of school. I never missed practice—I loved to practice. I loved to study. I loved school. I loved all the sports. I took the attitude of whatever is in front of you, you go and do that thing the best you can. My report card would be all A's, but that was because of all the nights I was at home alone doing my homework. It didn't matter if it was school, sports, or digging a ditch. I just enjoyed the feeling of accomplishing something and doing it to the best of my ability.

"It's hard to say exactly where you get a specific trait. I think some are innate characteristics that you're born with, and some are learned characteristics that you pick up from your environment. With our kids, at an early age, it was easy to see that they came programmed with a lot of different aspects of personality, and that was clear to my wife and me. When you're born, you come into the world with a certain package of inborn traits, and I think the environmental issues kind of take over from there. It's hard to say where that starts and stops, but both of those aspects are very important.

"As for me, by the time I was around twelve, my value systems were pretty much in place. I respected people. I knew you had to work hard to accomplish what you wanted and that there were no short cuts. I always had a strong sense of honesty. My dad taught me that.

"To me, the word fun in sports is a very, very relative term. I enjoyed achieving things and doing things I didn't think I could do. So, if that's fun, I had a lot of it. I remember when I was frustrated with playing, my dad would always say you've just got to have fun. That was kind of an easy way to describe what was going on and didn't really address the situation for me. Here I was doing something that was hard and challenging for me, something I really wanted to succeed at. Getting it done was the reward. Fun, to me, was the satisfaction of achieving something.

"My dad was a good college athlete. He played at BYU, but I never knew that he was all-conference and a standout athlete. He didn't want to pressure me to be great or think that I had to follow in his footsteps. He just didn't want me to be a quitter. I don't think it mattered to him if I was great or not; he just wanted me to do the best I could. To him, if you went to class every day and did the best you could do, and still got low grades, that was still okay. You gave your best effort, and that was the important thing. He may not be completely satisfied, but his attitude would be that now there's room for improvement.

"I've refereed and been involved with Little League games now for some time. It's just awful to watch some parents who believe that their kid is going to fulfill some kind of sports fantasy. They teach their kids that the satisfaction is not in doing your best, but in being great. Then, if you're not great, you haven't dignified your efforts. There's something really sick about that. There has to be some point where the effort is enough. If you're not great at it, that's got to be okay. To my dad, you were great if you gave it everything you had. That was his standard. He didn't care if you struck out ten times as long as you gave it your best effort and didn't quit. If you did that, to him, you were a phenomenal player.

"Parents who have in their minds that their child has a future in sports, and that's why they're playing, to me are abusive and negligent. Professional, college, and even high school sports have to be about excelling at your own pace. If a kid is fortunate enough to have the skill sets to move up the ladder, sports will find him/her. Sports should be a great teacher, and it should be fun. No matter how you look at your definition of fun, be it achievement or just purely fun, sports should be for the person playing it, not some vicarious dance. Parents should be supportive and not have an end in mind. The lesson is not how great your kid is, how fast they can run, or how far they can throw the ball. So many kids have been battered by those kinds of messed-up expectations. The expectation should be to do your best. If you strike out five times and in the next game you only strike out four times, that's a good reason to go to Dairy Queen.

"The guys who I played professional football with, and I know their history so I can speak to it, didn't have to deal with unreasonable expectations from their parents. It seems like the guys who thrived just played the game with the mindset that they were going to do their best and enjoy the experience. The guys who grew up with unrealistic expectations went against it, fought against it, or quit because they could never live up to the expectation. If you're playing for the right reason, it allows you a certain freedom to have a good experience. If you've got parents pushing kids to play, especially under the wrong set of expectations, the game becomes a burden, and the child usually loses the opportunity to participate in the wonderful lessons—lessons that an athlete will carry with them their entire life—that organized sports can provide."

* * *

Robert Schuller once said, "Spectacular achievement is always preceded by unspectacular preparation." That's true in any area of life. When people rise to the top of their particular game, in sports, life, or work, you can bet that there were months and years of unspectacular preparation involved in getting to where they got.

One of the common attributes of successful people is that they constantly give their best effort and are consistently trying to improve on their previous efforts. They may not be too thrilled with the various tasks they have to perform to prepare themselves, but they still do them to the best of their ability, understanding that this is the price they must pay to achieve their desired outcome. And that's a key dividing line between success and the lack thereof—successful folks are willing to do the things that other people aren't willing to do.

There's an old story about an elderly man sitting on his porch in his rocking chair, reflecting on the past and assessing his life accomplishments. The question is, do you want to take your seat in the rocking chair and think about all the things you wish you had done, or would you rather reflect on your life knowing that you took some chances and gave the best effort you were capable of?

Like the great hockey player, Wayne Gretzky, once said, "You miss 100 percent of the shots you never take." From the view in the rocking chair, you've either got some degree of satisfaction with what you've done, or you've got some degree of remorse for not doing, or not giving, your best effort.

Somewhere along the way, Steve Young embraced achievement as one of his primary motives in life. Maybe he was born with this trait, or maybe he acquired it from his environment. Regardless of where he got it, he certainly incorporated it into every aspect of his life. Whatever he might do, he was going to do it as best he could.

It's not the extraordinary athletic skills that Steve Young had that made him a Hall of Fame quarterback. It was the fervor he possessed to do whatever he was doing to the best of his ability. Maybe Steve Young had a vision of himself as a professional football player that helped him become a star player, or maybe what he became was simply a natural outcome of his desire to do whatever he was doing to the best of his ability. When you have that kind of attitude, all the other stuff tends to take care of itself.

Chapter 23

THE ROAD TO GREATNESS

I t has been a rewarding experience compiling, editing and writing *Pigskin Dreams*. It's also been a process that often tests your perseverance and commitment. Writing is a challenging and sometimes painful exercise. There are a million distractions amid a million thoughts and countless obligations that create significant barriers to completion. But completion is the gem—the jewel you've been digging for with pick and shovel, and alas, it's done. You're finished. That's the part we like most. That's where a sense of accomplishment and a degree of satisfaction surface to make the struggle and effort well worth it. That feels really good. It's a feeling you can only get from going through a process and reaching the end of that process, and the more difficult the process, the greater the degree of satisfaction.

It occurs to me that the preceding paragraph is probably an accurate representation of what many people go through in many aspects of life. There are frequently barriers and obstacles one has to overcome to reach a certain destination or goal. Take football, for example. Two-a-day practices in the summer heat probably don't top the list of ideal vacation locations. If the National Football League drafted new policies that cancelled all the two-a-days, I doubt that the players would stage a strike demanding that two-a-days be re-implemented.

While there may be some players who like the summer practices, it's a good bet that the vast majority view them as part of the process that has to be endured to achieve the performance levels they seek. The best part about two-a-days is when they're over and the player gets the opportunity to look back on his efforts and say, "I worked my tail off, and I'm as ready as anybody now."

Other areas of life reveal the same kind of thing. If you want to keep your home in ship-shape condition, you may have to do some things you don't necessarily want to do. But, when the house is clean, you're happy about it. If you want to do well in school, you have to hit the books, pay attention in class, and develop the right attitude about learning. When you get top marks in your class, you're pretty happy with yourself, even though you may not have enjoyed all the work you had to do. And if you're in business and want to increase your productivity, it may require that you get to the office a little earlier, call a few more customers, or learn some new skills to move from where you presently are to where you want to go.

Perhaps the tasks you have to incorporate into your schedule to accomplish your goals are not exactly the things you want to be doing, but when you get to your destination, you get to experience a level of satisfaction that's not available until you complete those difficult and challenging tasks.

Like many others have surmised in the past, perhaps it's all about pleasure and pain. We tend to do the things that produce pleasure and avoid the things that produce pain. In the case of the student who wants good grades and understands that the accomplishment of such will produce pleasure, sometimes the application of the efforts to obtain those goals are perceived as painful. After all, in the immediate, short-term sense, it's much more pleasurable to watch your favorite television show than to complete fifty algebra problems. But, for those who persevere, the pay-off is well worth the effort, and what may have been perceived as painful suddenly becomes recognized as the activity that actually created a pleasurable result.

There is a certain line of demarcation drawn in the sands of accomplishment that many people have a great challenge crossing. Most people want to succeed, but many don't have the right tools in their toolbox to build the bridge that crosses the line between success and the lack thereof. Somebody forgot to put a hammer in some of the toolboxes, and now, when you need the hammer to build the bridge, you're inadequately furnished with the proper tool to nail the planks across the bridge for you to cross. Seemingly, you're stuck on the backside of success and happiness, unable to cross that line of demarcation. Simply put, though, if that is your estimation of your circumstance, you're right. You are stuck. Your belief about your circumstance makes the reality of that circumstance your reality—bred, fed, and fostered by you.

Ultimately, it's your choice as to what you will or will not accomplish. That's a bitter pill to swallow for many folks. The hard fact is that another person can't do the things for you that you must do for yourself to move in the direction you desire to travel. If you cheat on a test, you get nothing of value in return that helps you move forward to a next level. If you drag around in practice, giving less than optimal effort, you'll reproduce that performance in the game. If you produce minimal efforts in your job, your rewards will be commensurate with those efforts.

It's all about the Law of Attraction and the cause and effect relationships that surround the Law of Attraction. For every thing (effect) that happens in your life, there's always a reason (cause). Your outcomes—your effects—can be traced back to certain choices you made at some point. Those choices resulted in some kind of action you took, and those actions resulted in some kind of outcome that manifested as a result of your choices and actions. If you chose not to do the algebra homework, you didn't cause your grade to be as good as you would have liked it to be. You cause your results to happen.

Much has been written and discussed about the Law of Attraction. A simple definition of the law would be that you attract the things into your life that you give your focus, energy, and attention to. For example, assume a young lady has developed a high degree of respect for herself and others. Along the way she developed a strong sense of obligation and duty to do the best she could do at whatever task she undertook. She decided that she would greet each day with enthusiasm, happiness, and persistence, understanding that she had the power to choose between the luminescence of a positive disposition or the darkness of a depressed and defeating demeanor.

Along her way, it was as if a shimmering, radiant glow shone on all that crossed her path, and those that broached the illumination of the emanating glow fell prey to some uplifting presence, perhaps unaware of the origin of the glow, but acutely aware that some phenomenon had implanted itself upon the psyche of the passerby whereby the fellow human being, for reasons unknown to him, had somehow been lifted up as he brushed against the radiant persona of the vibrant young lady on an ordinary sidewalk in an ordinary town.

What occurred is a perfect example of the Law of Attraction. It was the intention of the young lady to indelibly exude her positive characteristics in order that she might attract to herself the things that she desired and valued most. The things she held in her thoughts and the things she did in her actions combined to cause the young man to turn around and hurriedly catch up with the young lady and say, "Hi, my name is Tom. I know it sounds crazy, but I think I'm supposed to meet you. May I buy you a cup of coffee?"

Within the fateful twinkle of a shared gaze, years of attention, energy, and focus found purchase in the kindred hearts of the pair whose similar paths dissolved into a single intention. Destiny walked up and met them that day. Unlike many who never even notice destiny lurking beside them a simple blink away, they opened the door and embraced their destiny.

Conversely, another story reveals how The Law of Attraction works just as effectively at attracting negative circumstance into a life. For instance, suppose a person always finds reason to bestow blame for their circumstance on external factors but never assumes responsibility for their circumstances themselves. "If this had not happened, I would be so much better off...If I had the same breaks that he did, I'd be as lucky as he...That's just the way I am, I can't do anything about it...The teacher is awful and that's why I'm doing so bad in her class..."

There's an endless cacophony of excuses, guilty cohorts, sour circumstances, and perceived injustices from those who would be victim to their circumstance. The negative emotions paint directions for the subconscious mind to fulfill a destiny, as your destiny unfolds on the canvas of life. Thought correlates with its object. If you fill your thoughts with fear, jealousy, hatred, anxiety, and limitation, those will become the objects you realize and what you'll attract. If you align your thoughts, emotions, and beliefs as loftier aspirations and hold those visions steadfast in your mind, you will, likewise, attract those things into your life.

People who are successful in life didn't just happen to be in the right place at the right time. Sure, some folks have better opportunities and circumstances in their lives. And then there are others who are born into poverties of family, finance and faith. Regardless of what circumstance you're born into, and what circumstance you're surrounded by, there's a point where a person makes a choice and understands that the images and thoughts that occupy their mind are the starting point for their dreams and aspirations to be realized. Circumstance doesn't compose your destiny. It reveals it. You write your own music, and the tune you sing carries you up or drags you down.

The players included in *Pigskin Dreams* are perfect examples of the power of cause and effect. Undeniably, these players have more natural athletic ability than most of us do, but it's not the increased physical prowess they possessed that propelled them to the pinnacle of their profession. Any one of them will tell you that they all knew kids and teammates who were bigger, faster, and stronger.

At some point, these players made a choice that they would pursue their vocation with their maximum mental and physical capabilities. They weren't making excuses. They were blazing a trail that led to the realization of their untold potential. Did they have help along the way? Certainly, they did. Parents, teachers, peers, and coaches all contributed through the positive influences that they imparted upon these players. But ultimately it was up to the player to decide, with unrelenting conviction, that they were going to muster all their energies and powers to focus on becoming the best they could be and do the things necessary to accomplish that feat. They made a choice. They effected outcomes. They created their own destinies through their choices, actions, and intentions.

Everyone has the same opportunity to make a choice. Everyone has the power to make a choice. In fact, choice is one of the few constants in life. At any given moment, you're making a choice to do a thing or not do a thing. Even if you think that you're not making a choice, you still are. For example, maybe you've been thinking about exercising to get in better shape. You might say to yourself that you're thinking about doing that, but what you've really done is choose not to start exercising. Either way, good or bad, plus or minus, black or white, you've made a choice. You can't escape the necessity of choice. It lurks behind every thought and weaves your reality, thread by thread, into your destiny.

While choice ultimately defines who you are and what you accomplish, the influences you have in your life certainly play a major role in the way you view the world and the way you make your choices. If you didn't receive certain developmental things as an infant or child, there's a good chance that those omissions will have a negative impact on your ability to process your circumstances in an efficient and rewarding way. For example, if you had a mother who never held and loved you, who constantly screamed at you and left you isolated in another room, you're going to be at a distinct disadvantage when it comes to having meaningful relationships that require the ability to show and receive love.

There are certain requirements and phases that one needs to complete to successfully negotiate the challenging road of life. Life is a matrix, where earlier phases and conditions of your life constitute different points from which future capacities and abilities originate, take form, or develop. For example, as an infant, if you didn't receive the love, affection, and attention you needed, you'll have more of a challenge fitting into the social norms of society. You missed that lesson, so to speak. Because that's such a critical formative step in development, it's much more difficult for you to build from that particular point and develop the skills and tools you need to successfully move into a new phase of life. But it doesn't make it impossible.

Humans are the only animals that require such a long-term parenting experience. In fact, we're essentially helpless when it comes to the first few years of our life, relying on our mothers (or primary caretakers) to supply us with all those things we need to survive and develop knowledge about the world around us.

For about the first seven years of life, from the safety and security of the mother's bond, we develop an understanding and knowledge of our world, and the degree of input that the mother (and others) imparts during this time is critical to the image we have about ourselves, the world around us, and the way we operate in that world. To optimally complete this early phase of life, the caretakers must provide necessary things. They must protect and nurture the child, while at the same time allowing the child to explore, discover, and develop newfound capabilities.

Understandably, in this early phase of life there isn't that much complex decision-making going on in the infant's or young child's mind. Mentally, they simply haven't developed the neural pathways that give us humans the blessing or curse of higher reasoning. But, as children grow, they start developing more complex neural networks in their brains that signify movement into another phase of life. From about seven to eleven years, children become more cognizant of their own power and volition, and they start to understand and develop skills for survival in their world and begin a sort of independent detachment from the earlier maternal matrix they are now exiting.

By the time adolescence rolls around, independence and the feeling of self-awareness begin to dominate. More abstract thinking occurs, and with an interconnection to and dependence upon earlier phases, provides the basis for how the adolescent processes the world and how they see themselves beginning to fit into the world.

As maturity continues its progression, the mind plays an increasingly important role in defining what your reality is. At some point in the development of *you,* the solid foundations of your realities formed in the protective environments of the earlier phases of your life give way or yield to the processes of your thought. Now, all that has come before simply provides a stepping-stone or foundation for you to use your mind and your thought to condition your brain to see things as you instruct the brain to see them. Thought becomes reality, limited only by your self-imposed limitations.

Throughout the stories in *Pigskin Dreams,* you see repeating themes common to the players. There was always a significant caregiver present to provide the critical building blocks for the nurturing and safety of the child. Whether from a rich or poor family, single or married household, there were caregivers, in one form or another, present to provide the critical stability and attention the infant and toddler needed.

As youngsters, these players had the opportunity to participate in many play-related activities in parks, in different leagues, with friends or family members. Play is a critically important component of development. According to many experts, play in the formative years is one of the most important things children can do to help them develop their creativity, imagination, and physical ability. Play is where kids learn to build their environment, mimic adult roles, strategize, take risks, learn new skills, make mistakes, and solve problems.

Throughout history, in any given society, play has been a central theme that enabled children to learn about the norms of their society and how to operate in that society. Play prepared Native American children to become successful warriors and hunters. Play prepared the Greek child to become the soldier or senator. Even today, the simple game of a little girl's tea party, or a little boy's game of dodge ball, and a million other examples of play, serve as the formative foundations for how a child thinks about himself/herself in society and how he/she will ultimately operate in that society. And, the more a child engages in play-related activities, the more opportunity that child has to develop the critical attributes that enable the child to express greater degrees of their potential.

Another critical component to the success of these players is the presence of a difference-maker in their lives. A difference-maker is anyone who had a profound influence and caused, or helped initiate, a difference in thinking. Howie Long had a great example of a difference-maker when the high school coach came up to him in the hallway of his new school and asked if he had ever played football. Even though Howie had never participated in any organized sports, he answered, "Oh yeah, I've played." In an instant the world changed for Howie that day in the hall.

Kellen Winslow also had a great example of difference-makers in his life. When Kellen was a junior in high school, football wasn't even on his radar screen, and he had never even played on an organized level. He had a job with UPS and had already crafted plans to continue his education after high school.

Recognizing the athletic prowess that Kellen exhibited in gym class, the football coaches had another plan. They worked on Kellen for weeks trying to get him to understand the opportunity that lay before him as a football player. While we're sure the coaches wanted Kellen for the benefit of the team, it's equally as evident that the coaches' prime motives were more about helping a kid understand the op-portunities that he had. A single moment of decision—a second in time—changed the entire course of Kellen Winslow's life, and it likely would have never gone that direction but for the actions of the differ-ence-makers in his life.

Perhaps three of the most critical components to success, in sports or in life, reside in the caregiver's ability to provide a nurturing envi-ronment for a child, the opportunity for children to engage in all kinds of play-related activities, and the presence of difference-makers in a child's life. Why would these be such critical requirements for suc-cess? Because the decisions, momentous or miniscule, people make in their lives are determined primarily from the ingrained dispositions and habits that they develop from their environment, which affect their thoughts, which lead to words, actions, habits, and the formation of character.

From the central reality of *your character*, you assess and estimate your world and circumstance and make choices about that world to ultimately define the direction you choose to travel and the awaiting destiny you create.

Think. Say. Do. Be.™ In the simplest of terms, that's the secret to success—on the field, in the office, in the classroom or in life. We are what we repeatedly do, as Aristotle put it. And, what we repeatedly do is predicated on what we repeatedly think and what we repeatedly say. Thinking, saying, and doing create the habits of our thought and the way we view our circumstances and make decisions about our circumstances. And, from those habits of thought, your character is formed and revealed.

If you're not happy about where you presently are in life, you simply need to change your point of view and take some kind of new action to propel you in a new direction. You need new habits to ascend to new horizons, and those habits originate with the thoughts in your mind. As James Allen once wrote: "Alter your outlook upon life, and your outward life will alter."

There are only two baseline choices people can make in their life. Choices are either constructive or destructive. That's the bottomline barometer of life. You build up or you tear down. You ascend or you descend. You move forward or backward. You choose plus or you choose minus. You can blame your circumstances, your disadvantages, or other people, but at some point, it all comes down to you and the decisions you make.

The world we see isn't the world we see with our eyes. It's the world we see with our mind. The players in *Pigskin Dreams* saw an image of greatness in their minds and coordinated their intentions and actions with that image, and rose to the highest levels of their profession. They achieved their status through the direct application of their character to their particular circumstances. Through their strength of character, these men created their destinies.

And we all will achieve our destinies. They may be grand or they may not. But make no mistake, they will be our destinies, forged by the intent and actions we possess and pursue and the image we hold in our minds about the possibilities that life holds for us.

About the Authors

About the Authors

*E*very life has certain foundational components that help define the ultimate character of an individual. The authors believe that *Pigskin Dreams* shows inspiring examples of this principle and can help encourage a greater awareness of the importance of developing positive character traits enabling a more fulfilling, rewarding life.

Dr. Stephen Below is a fourth-generation chiropractor. He is the co-founder and CEO of the largest chiropractic consumer membership organization in the world, Preferred Chiropractic Doctor; founder

and publisher of Wellness Bound Publications; founder and CEO of the national non-profit organization, the Community Wellness Alliance; entrepreneur; national speaker, and writer. Dr. Below lives in Alabama with his wife and four children.

Dr. Stephen Below

Todd Kalis is an eight-year veteran of the National Football League. He played for the Minnesota Vikings, Cincinnati Bengals and Pittsburgh Steelers. He is currently president of the Pittsburgh chapter, chairman of the Board of Chapter Presidents and vice-chairman of the

Todd A. Kalis

Board of Directors of the National Football League Alumni. Mr. Kalis is also a business development executive in the Pittsburgh area. He lives in Cranberry Township, Pennsylvania, with his wife and three children.